W9-ADN-939

WITHDRAWN
L. R. COLLEGE LIBRARY

Beyond Atonement

Marie von Ebner-Eschenbach

Beyond Atonement

Translated and with an introduction
by
Vanessa Van Ornam

CARL A. RUDISILL LIBRARY
LENOIR-RHYNE COLLEGE

CAMDEN HOUSE

Translator and publisher would like to express their heartfelt gratitude to the
Austrian Cultural Institute New York
and to the Austrian Ministry for Foreign Affairs
for their generous financial support for this book and for its companion volume, the
translation of Ebner-Eschenbach's *Their Pavel* (original title *Das Gemeindekind*),
translated by Lynne Tatlock and published in 1996 by Camden House.

Copyright © 1997 by
CAMDEN HOUSE, INC.

All rights reserved, including the right of reproduction
in whole or in part in electronic or any other form.
All rights to this publication will be vigorously defended.

PT
1853
.U5713
1997
Jene/1998

Published by Camden House, Inc.
Drawer 2025
Columbia, SC 29202 USA

Printed on acid-free paper.
Binding materials are chosen for strength and
durability.

All Rights Reserved
Printed in the United States of America
First Edition

ISBN: 1–57113–113–2

Library of Congress Cataloging-in-Publication Data

Ebner-Eschenbach, Marie von, 1830–1916.
  [Unsühnbar. English]
  Beyond atonement / Marie von Ebner-Eschenbach; translated by
Vanessa Van Ornam.
        p.   cm. – (Studies in German literature, linguistics, and
culture)
    Includes bibliographical references.
    ISBN 1–57113–113–2 (alk. paper)
    I. Van Ornam, Vanessa, 1957–   . II. Title. III. Series: Studies
in German literature, linguistics, and culture (Unnumbered).
    PT1853.U5713   1996
    833'.8—dc20   96–42230
                                                         CIP

Acknowledgments

I would like first to acknowledge the work of the translator of an early edition of *Beyond Atonement*, Mary Robinson, whose translation appeared in 1892. Fidelity to Ebner's text was greatly facilitated by Robinson's work; as the author's contemporary, she had greater access to terms describing articles that have disappeared in the twentieth century. I am also indebted to her for what are presumably her own translations of two verses that appear at the end of Chapter 12 and Chapter 14. I am particularly grateful to her for her choice of a title. The literal translation of the title, "Inexpiable," does not leap off the shelf into the arms of an eager reader, and I am pleased to have been spared it. As a title, "Beyond Atonement" captures the melodramatic tenor of a novel that features not only the demonic seducer of a virtuous woman, but a profligate illegitimate brother, a mad mother, angelic children, and two deaths by drowning. I hope these plot elements explain part of the novel's appeal to readers. I myself am profoundly grateful for having been introduced to this text by Lynne Tatlock's seminar on the construction of gender in nineteenth-century literature. My gratitude in general to Lynne Tatlock for her suggestion that I work on this text and for the constant, insightful, and generous help she has given me in my work on the translation is almost inexpressible, but I hope this acknowledgment may begin to communicate even a part of my thanks. This translation literally would not exist without her. It also would not exist without James Hardin, Camden House, and Washington University. I am grateful to James Hardin and Camden House for undertaking the publication of translations of this and other wonderful texts by Marie von Ebner-Eschenbach and to Washington University for generously supporting this project. Thanks also to Carol Jenkins for her knowledgeable help with terms relating to equestrian equipment, a bewildering field indeed. I also wish to thank Hans-Jürgen Homann for his constant willingness to explore, explain, and agonize with me over the nuances and alternatives expressed in the original German. Finally, I would like to thank my parents, Georgia Van Ornam and Robert Van Ornam, for their unquestioning support and encouragement of whatever I have undertaken over the years. I dedicate this translation to them.

Introduction

Marie von Ebner-Eschenbach (1830–1916) was celebrated even in her own life-time as Austria's foremost nineteenth-century woman writer; yet her work was sometimes subject to harsh critical reception. The novel *Beyond Atonement*, seri-alized in the *Deutsche Rundschau* in 1889, received notably ambivalent reviews. The text was based loosely on an event that had actually taken place years ear-lier in an aristocratic Austrian family. A woman had announced after the death of her husband that the apparent heir to the estate was in fact not the son of her deceased spouse. Since the law would continue to recognize the "legitimacy" of any child born to a married woman, the family, with the consent of the son, al-tered the line of succession to the estate. The former heir continued to live in perfect harmony with all the members of the family.[1] Most contemporary critics asserted that Ebner had insufficiently motivated her heroine's seduction and subsequent behavior; the critics insisted that these were inconsistent with the protagonist's character as a woman of noble sensibilities with a strong sense of justice. Ebner took the criticism to heart and changed her text significantly over the course of the nine editions published in her lifetime. Some of her critics were mollified; others remained unconvinced. The changes she made present the marital "happiness" of the heroine, Maria, in a more subdued light, refashion the seducer, Tessin, into a more demonically attractive figure and keep him linger-ing in the heroine's thoughts in the early years of her marriage, and allow Maria to discover that her father had withheld from her an early proposal of marriage from Tessin.[2] Ebner also has her heroine display more resistance to her own se-duction, while the narrative emphasizes the character's subservience to the patrilineal inheritance she could have violated: dialogue added to the scene in which her dead husband's will is read underscores the law's acceptance of any child born in wedlock as legitimate.[3] Discussions about the plausibility of the protagonist's actions, however, have continued even up to the present. Then and now, many critics have been unable to reconcile Maria's laudable character with what they term her disregard for her marital and maternal obligations. Un-favorable comparisons of this novel to other novels of adultery suggest that al-though a reviewer might expect some women to succumb to seduction, this par-ticular wife and mother should not have been susceptible. Ebner's own reply to the complaint of these "Philistines" was that only remorse had made Maria into the noble figure she became before her death.[4]

Despite the skepticism of some, however, the novel is generally acknowl-edged to number among Ebner's best works; from the beginning critics have praised its literary artistry as well as its brilliantly evocative portrait of the Aus-trian aristocracy. As a member of this class, Ebner was well acquainted with its history, its preoccupations, its strengths, and its weaknesses. The end of feudalism and the rise of liberalism before and after the revolution of 1848 had contributed to a decline from which the Austrian aristocracy never recovered; it had outlived its way of life, a fact that many of its representatives failed to recognize.

Ebner's portraits of the Austrian upper class were frequently less than flattering. One early critic of *Byond Atonement*, for instance, took umbrage at what he called Ebner's "constant" mocking of the Austrian aristocracy as incompetent and useless. Among other things, he objected to this novel's portrayal of the Viennese *comtesses* — the young, unmarried daughters of aristocrats — in the ball scene of Chapter 9. He argued in their "defense" that these young women are open, healthy, courageous, and family-oriented, "despite being, like Americans, somewhat outspoken," that they become good wives and mothers when they marry, and that they are "ladies of high society, through and through." A subsequent reviewer, Moritz Necker, took issue with the first critic's comments and pointed out that his description of the Viennese *comtesses* might have come directly from Ebner's own novella *Komtesse Muschi* (1885).[5] The characterization of the novella's protagonist — a horse-loving, ill-educated, shallow *comtesse* — had inspired the indignation of the women it satirized; Ebner responded in verse: "I was criticized / For writing Muschi / I did it for the sake and the benefit of all Muschis."[6] In other words, even her censure of her class's behavior reveals her genuine affection for that class. Necker argued that Ebner directs her criticism not against the character of the *comtesses*, but against their ideals; her texts expose the "banal interests" of high society, which find their peak in sports and horse races.[7] *Beyond Atonement* explores a range of aristocratic behaviors; the text counters the thoughtless and superficial Wonsheims, for instance, with the solid, hard-working Wilhelms and suggests that the latter are a model that can redefine the role of the aristocracy. Ebner's fictional world mirrors its historical counterpart: the role of the aristocracy is in flux. With references to past and present objects, artifacts, issues, and luminaries, Ebner creates an atmosphere in which characters born to wealth and privilege are torn by the competing demands of nostalgia for the aristocracy's golden age, resistance to movements advocating social welfare, and the desire to participate in the useful work of the new era.

Like her heroine, the author was born to an aristocratic family in Moravia; her mother, her father's second wife, died two weeks later. Ebner's life was divided between summers on the family estate and winters in Vienna. She received what Gabriele Reuter called the typical upbringing of an Austrian *comtesse*: "a little learning, first with a bad governess and then with a good one, English and French speaking, a little needlework. Riding, dancing, shooting, and hunting, as chivalrous arts, done in competition with one's brothers, were indispensable to the education of children of the landed aristocracy."[8] What her peers did not share, however, was her desire to write. At fourteen, in fact, she had announced that she "wanted to become 'the greatest woman writer of all nations and ages' or die."[9] This goal brought her into conflict with her family; it was axiomatic that the aristocracy — particularly its women — did not become writers. In 1848, when she was eighteen, Ebner married her cousin Moritz, who was fifteen years her senior and who had given her writing early encouragement. He became less supportive, however, as she experienced one failure after another in her attempt to become a dramatist. She turned finally to prose narratives and in 1880 had her first big success with *Lotti, die Uhrmacherin* (*Lotti, the Watchmaker*). By 1900, at the age of seventy, she had reached the pinnacle of her literary fame.

One measure of that fame was the frequent comparison of Ebner's work to the novellas of Theodor Storm and Gottfried Keller. *Beyond Atonement* inspired comparisons to Fontane's *Effi Briest*, Tolstoy's *Anna Karenina*, and other now lesser-known novels of adultery, although even her fans generally concluded that Fontane's text was a better novel; Effi's flaws, and therefore her susceptibility to a seducer, were always more evident to her readers. The defects of the adulteress, however, are not the sole basis of the novel of female adultery.

Twentieth-century studies of the novel of adultery as a genre illuminate aspects of Ebner's text and its adulterous protagonist. Judith Armstrong's work on the nineteenth-century novel of adultery identifies a recurring plot trajectory.[10] These novels begin with an existing order — a marriage in conformity with western marital models — and then detail the disruption of the order by the adultery of one or both spouses. The narratives conclude with the reestablishment and vindication of the order, often accomplished through the death of the adulterous spouse and/or the narrative's introduction of other characters as participants in an exemplary marriage. The "arranged, the mistaken, the loveless marriage are always the guilty root-causes" of the wife's adultery; the wife then faces a conflict between "love and duty, freedom and obligation."[11] The fate shared by most of those who opt out of duty and obligation suggests that society has a stake in the preservation of the order it has established; the fictional adulteress is the exception who proves the rule.

Tony Tanner's study, on the other hand, suggests that the rule generates its own transgression.[12] The eighteenth and nineteenth centuries witnessed the growth of the contract as the mediator of human relations, and marriage was the contract on which other bonds were contingent. However, "contracts *create* transgressions; the two are inseparable, and the one would have no meaning without the other."[13] If the marriage contract forms the basis of the social contract, what undermines the former reveals the instability of the latter. It is therefore not coincidental that many of the century's "great" novels focus on adultery,[14] because of what is at stake for society in the adulterous act: if the social structure is founded upon marriage, then adultery undermines civilization itself. The novel of adultery recognizes and contributes to the instability of the social system by scrutinizing and exposing the self-destructive potential at the heart of the family on which other bonds are based.

Civilization's interest in prohibiting adultery suggests that at least the initial adulterous act will take place outside society's presumptive realm. Biblical guidelines for the sentencing of adulterers[15] suggest the metaphor of the city and the field to describe allegedly "social space" and "nonsocial space"; what happens in "nonsocial space" is to some extent outside the law.[16] The protagonists of the novel of adultery may attempt to live in the "field," but eventually discover that the existence of nonsocialized space is in fact illusory and that nowhere can they live outside society's proscriptions.[17] Maria's single adulterous act takes place in an eighteenth-century summerhouse on the grounds of her husband's estate; the site indicates a spatial separation from the manor house (and its order) of which she is mistress, and the reference to the eighteenth century evokes its frivolous mores, which contrast to nineteenth-century solidity and propriety.[18] Nevertheless, the representatives of the social order are never too far distant: her half-brother, Wolfi, enters the summerhouse with the news that he knows her secret, and Maria is able to summon help with her cries when Wolfi collapses. The additional metaphor of the temple, however, as the place in which society's representatives demand condemnation of the adulteress and are instructed to examine their own flaws instead, offers an escape from both the polarities of city and field and from the vast expanse of society's sphere of censorious influence. The novel of adultery can be a kind of "temple" that attempts to mediate the tensions between those inside, outside, and above the social structure.[19] *Beyond Atonement* takes on that task in its evocation of a saintly adulteress whose "fall" exposes only the flaws of the society she transcends.

Maria's case is further illuminated by the suggestion that adultery "introduces an agonizing and irresolvable category-confusion into the individual and thence into society itself," because it conflates categories that society insists should be separate: "wife and mother" and "mistress and lover."[20] Hence Maria's reluctance to be admired, to be thought honorable, when she feels dishonored and dishonorable. Society's response to this violation of categories can range from banishment of adulterers to a questioning of the law itself. The novel of adultery may thus articulate the tension between the two positions, exhibiting "a strictness that works to maintain the law, and a sympathy and understanding with the adulterous violator that works to undermine it."[21] With this tension in mind, Ebner's title may perhaps be read as a question: is Maria's transgression in fact "beyond atonement"? One friend offered the author his opinion that her novel had definitively proven that "certain crimes" indeed cannot be expiated,[22] but the text itself leaves the question unanswered. Ebner's stated interest, however, was in solving another puzzle. When she wrote to her publisher to offer him her manuscript, she said that, after hearing of the case that inspired her story, she had wondered what might have motivated a noble and universally admired woman to take the heroic action of destroying her own reputation for the sake of truth.[23]

The author's particular intention perhaps explains the difference between her novel and others of the same genre with which Ebner's readers — and the author herself — might have been familiar. She had, for instance, read *Anna Karenina* and liked it, although she felt that Tolstoy should have divided his material into two books.[24] She had probably also read Ossip Schubin's then well-known *"Gloria victis!"* After her own novel was published, a friend wrote to her that *Beyond Atonement* was far superior to both — but still found it less than plausible that Maria would have been unfaithful to her wonderful husband and heedless of the consequences to her son of her confession.[25] The differences between these three novels highlight the ways in which Ebner's narrative and protagonist diverge from the models found in other novels of the genre, which tend to fall into two basic categories.[26] The heroines of Schubin's novel, Achim von Arnim's *Armut, Reichtum, Schuld und Buße der Gräfin Dolores* (*The Poverty, Wealth, Sin and Penance of Countess Dolores*), and Goethe's *Die Wahlverwandtschaften* (*Elective Affinities*) each commit real or imagined adultery and suffer a crisis of conscience as a result; each, however, is permitted some form of atonement and all are spared the public confession. Although Schubin's heroine also longs to confess, she keeps her secret for the sake of her son. Neither *Anna Karenina*, Flaubert's *Madame Bovary*, Fontane's *Effi Briest*, nor Ferdinand von Saar's *Schloß Kostenitz* is concerned with the issue of atonement; the cuckolded husband of Fontane's novel in fact seems to address Ebner's text in his claim that there is no such thing as inexpiable guilt — time and a husband's love can erase all.

Ebner's contemporaries read *Beyond Atonement* in the context of *Effi Briest* and the many other novels of adultery their century had produced, judging the protagonist, her motivation, and the aesthetic qualities of the text against those other narratives. Combining the concepts of the restoration of order and the inevitability of a contract's transgression is useful to a reading of *Beyond Atonement* and other novels of the same genre. The order "restored" in these texts is an order now keenly aware of its own fragility and vulnerability. In addition to the many dead or suicidal adulteresses and lovers killed in duels, the "restoration" of order leaves in its wake disillusioned husbands and families and a society compelled to recognize, with the reader, that its contracts can be breached and its structures undermined. Although *Beyond Atonement*'s female protagonist denounces herself and dies a year later, she leaves virtually everyone in her social circle convinced of her fundamental goodness — which calls into question the conventional morality evident in her mother-in-law's condemnation — and has revealed the instability of a system of patrilineal inheritance dependent on the continuing cooperation of women who have been given in marriages of convenience.

Vanessa Van Ornam
St. Louis, Missouri, July 1996

Notes

[1] Burkhard Bittrich, ed., *Unsühnbar*, by Marie von Ebner-Eschenbach, Kritische Texte und Deutungen, no. 1 (Bonn: Bouvier, 1978), 235.

[2] Bittrich 263–66.

[3] Bittrich 247.

[4] Bittrich 242.

[5] Bittrich 250–51.

[6] Quoted in Karlheinz Rossbacher, "Das Debüt einer Schriftstellerin: Marie von Ebner-Eschenbachs Episteln *Aus Franzensbad*," *From Vormärz to Fin de Siècle: Essays in Nineteenth-Century Austrian Literature*, ed. Mark G. Ward (Blairgowree: Lochee, 1986), 58; my translation.

[7] Bittrich 252.

[8] Gabriele Reuter, *Ebner-Eschenbach* (Berlin: Schuster & Loeffler, n.d.), 13.

[9] Carl Steiner, *Of Reason and Love: The Life and Works of Marie von Ebner-Eschenbach (1830–1916)* (Riverside, CA: Ariadne P, 1994), 21.

[10] Judith Armstrong, *The Novel of Adultery* (London: Macmillan, 1976).

[11] Armstrong 65.

[12] Tony Tanner, *Adultery in the Novel: Contract and Transgression* (Baltimore: Johns Hopkins UP, 1979).

[13] Tanner 11.

[14] Tanner 11.

[15] Tanner (18–19) cites the Mosaic laws on adultery (Deuteronomy 22: 22–27), which distinguish between women whose illicit sex takes place in the city and those who are "forced" in the field: women in the city must have failed to cry for help and so are fully culpable and to be stoned, whereas women in the field could not be heard and thus are blameless. The "scribes and the Pharisees" (St. John 8: 3–11) refer to these laws when they bring a woman "taken in adultery" to the temple to receive Christ's judgment. He instructs those "without sin" to cast the first stone; one by one, they leave the temple (Tanner 20–22).

[16] Tanner 19.

[17] Tanner 23.

[18] Here it is interesting to note that Ebner countered her publisher's opposition to some of the character Aunt Dolph's speeches as too risqué by using as her excuse the more relaxed mores of the eighteenth-century women on whom Dolph models herself (Bittrich 240).

[19] Tanner 23–24.

[20] Tanner 12–13.

[21] Tanner 14.

[22] Bittrich 249.

[23] Bittrich 235.

[24] Bittrich 236.

[25] Bittrich 243.

[26] The following is based on Bittrich's (345–50) discussion of these novels.

Translator's Note

The first translation of this novel into English was done by Mary Robinson and was published in 1892 by Hurst & Company in New York. Robinson's translation was based on the first or second (the two are identical) edition of Ebner's text and thus does not contain most of the changes the author made (primarily in the third edition) in order to add psychological credibility to the protagonist's actions. My own translation is based on the eighth edition, published in 1908,[1] which is the last one known with any certainty to have been revised by the author herself, although there is some evidence that she also undertook the few stylistic revisions of the ninth edition as well.[2] While the first translation strives for a fidelity to the text that sometimes results in rather wooden English prose, I have attempted to translate with an English-speaking reader's expectations in mind. I have, however, also tried to retain something of the late nineteenth-century flavor of the novel, which explains lexical choices such as "writing-case" and "toothpowder"; an updating of these terms would introduce undesirable anachronisms into the text. Burkhard Bittrich demonstrates that Ebner's own modifications of her text tended toward more precision and the substitution of more commonly used words for the less familiar. She also replaced most of the originally foreign words with German equivalents, which results in a more accessible text, as does the progressively less complicated syntax. Her introduction of commas into the first book version of her story was apparently intended to force pauses, which I read as part of her attempt to simplify her sentences for readers. These were retained through the third edition and, although many were later removed in editions that were edited only by the publisher, I have used them liberally as well for the same reason. I hope that in other respects, too, I have been faithful to the author's own tendencies in revision, and I am grateful for Bittrich's painstaking work in documenting those revisions.

[1] Marie von Ebner-Eschenbach, *Unsühnbar* (Berlin: Paetel, 1908).

[2] Burkhard Bittrich, ed., *Unsühnbar*, by Marie von Ebner-Eschenbach, Kritische Texte und Deutungen, no. 1 (Bonn: Bouvier, 1978), 287–88.

I.

The performance of *Fidelio* had ended; the audience streamed out of the opera house and dispersed quickly in all directions. Snow had fallen for the last twenty-four hours, diligently, incessantly, in large flakes; it lay heavily on the roofs, veiled the light of the street lamps, and made the work of the snow shovelers almost useless. Coaches rolled up silently; men and women wrapped in furs climbed into the plushly upholstered carriages. Several shop clerks helped their lightly clad lovelies into a hack with broken windows. As swiftly as the wind, one cab after another dashed away. Their hats tilted to one side, their moustaches waxed, the owners of the "smart rigs" sat on the coachman's box bent slightly forward, a rein in each hand. Their horses took off, exerting all their strength and vitality in order to bring callow heirs of the landed gentry, highborn cavalry officers, and sportsmen as quickly as possible to the casino of the Jockey Club. Forced to the edge of the street, crowded omnibuses pulled by worn-out nags and driven by sleepy coachmen rumbled toward the suburbs of the city. Respectable middle-class families, wrapped up warmly and with heightened appetite — one gets so hungry at the theater — went home to a hearty dinner or made their way to a restaurant.

Disregarding the nasty weather, several infantry officers strolled leisurely toward the nearest cafe. They were a small troop, but eager for action and sure of conquest. They spoke of the fashionable ladies in the theater boxes and of the ballet dancers and the horses of people they knew. They were joined by a "one-year volunteer,"[1] the son of a banker who had received a title of nobility, who liked to say, "We cavaliers" and "We of the racetrack." He kept quiet about the fact that the chair in his father's counting-house was the only steed he had ever mounted with any feeling of security.

The gentlemen were passed by a young teacher, who was quickly making her way homeward. Her coat was threadbare, but she was not cold; her way was long and lonely, but she was not afraid. She was reveling in the bliss she had just experienced, the bliss of the connoisseur. There were, after all, hours of the most sublime exaltation even in her harsh and difficult existence. The strength that she had drawn from them would have to last her a long time. Those who must purchase manna for the soul at the expense of their daily bread cannot afford this sweet refreshment often.

On Operngasse, a crew of workers was busy erecting a pyramid of snow when a brougham drawn by thoroughbreds came by at a ceremonial trot. The flame of a gas lamp illuminated the interior of the carriage for a moment. Two ladies sat inside it, the one old and of a sickly appearance, in a dark hood and wrap, the other very young, very beautiful, bareheaded, with a classic profile, taller by a head than her companion.

"Hey!" cried the fat coachman in a casual warning to the streetsweepers, and they all stepped back — with one exception. This one jumped in front of the coach, looked up at the driver with mocking familiarity, and forced him to swerve, which he did without turning his head, while the footman beside him murmured, "Back from America, and a streetsweeper? Don't they have that sort of job there?"

"Sure," came the answer. "But that wouldn't serve his purpose. He wants to be here spying on us and causing trouble, the scoundrel."

This remark was aimed at a tall, slender young man with a pale face, sunken cheeks, and large dark brown eyes. He wore tattered clothes; his small hat, full of holes, was pushed back, exposing his face and his features, which were still attractive despite the degeneracy they expressed. With insolent ease, he drew himself up in the glow of the street lamp and, staring brazenly at the young lady whose head was bent toward the carriage window, presented his broom before her as though it were a rifle.

The carriage drove on and the workers laughed. "Look at Wolfi!" Wolfi, pretending to be angry, cried, "Riffraff! What are you laughing at? What have I done? I've rendered military honors. To whom? To Countess Maria Wolfsberg, my — my dear relative."

The one so designated had not changed expression at the laborer's gesture, but she colored a little and said to her companion in an uneasy tone, "Aunt Dolph, did you see that man? Wearing a torn summer coat and cracked shoes in this cold weather . . . ."

"Oh, my dear, he's had his liquor; he's warmer than I am," replied her aunt, shivering.

"Did you see what he did?"

"Oh, yes — a joker."

"He's no joker — he's an enemy who hates us."

The countess interrupted her. "Stop it. You're nervous. At your age you don't yet have the right to be. A drunk permits himself a joke — what of it? We see it if it amuses us; we do not see it if it annoys us. It's morbid to reflect on it."

Maria was silent. She did not enjoy arguing with her aunt, because she always got the worst of it. The countess was shrewd and quick-witted; her brother, Count Wolfsberg, even called her wise and honored his sister, many years older than he, as a confidant, an advisor, and a friend. She, on the other hand, loved nothing in the world so much as him. Sickly since her youth and of an independent nature, she had never felt herself called to marriage and had, without inner conflict, rejected one after another the many suitors for her plain person and her brilliant fortune. Countess Adolphine or Dolph, as she was called by the family, had long lived on her estate, devoting herself to the care of her rheumatism and her fortune, which she intended to leave, significantly increased, to her brother. When this brother became a widower, she made a great sacrifice for him in acquiescing to his request: she renounced the independence of her own household and took over the management of his. When the time came to introduce Maria into society, she did even more: she gave up the comfort and tranquillity she found so necessary and kept watch many a night at the ball, her aching head bejeweled with diamonds, and in finery so unbecoming to her that not even her maid ventured to compliment her. She was horribly bored by these occasions, bored even when she was superbly entertaining others with her sharp and scintillating wit. "Lucky Bertrand de Born," she would say, "who at least needed half his intellect. I would be happy if I could find takers for even a tenth of mine!"[2]

When they arrived at home, the countess retired to her rooms, while Maria entered the drawing room of her own apartments. There, each evening, she awaited an honored guest — her father. She almost never waited in vain. Although the high government position he occupied and the love of pleasure he found no reason not to indulge left him little spare time, he managed to keep free for Maria the last hour of her day.

She now allowed her maid to take her opera cloak and began immediately to prepare tea, for which everything necessary had been placed on a small table near the sideboard.

Maria took great care with her preparations. In offering him a cup of tea, she had fulfilled all the filial duties her father expected of her. It would have been her ardent desire to do something for him, to be able to be something to him, but she felt that the notion of such an ambition in his daughter's heart would have made him laugh. He wanted to see her cheerful and happy, and when she had answered his questions — "Did you enjoy yourself?" "Do you like this?" "Do you like that?" — in the affirmative, his customarily stern and serious expression would lighten. Thanks to his generosity, she had been able to transform her apartments into a small museum; should it occur to her, however, while admiring a picture or a bronze, to reveal anything of her newly acquired knowledge of art history, his expression would become so mocking that Maria would fall silent in confusion and feel humiliatingly foolish. As for the costly Blüthner[3] with which he had recently surprised her and which stood in the corner wrapped in soft Indian cloth, she had not yet been allowed to play anything but operetta and dance music on it for the benefactor. She had not been easy to discourage, she had always found a transition from the trivial to the beautiful, from the amusing to the uplifting — but after just the first few notes she would hear the dreaded "Good night, Maria" and the count would have disappeared from the room. On such occasions she did not stop playing; it would have annoyed him greatly, he who protested against special consideration for himself as another would have against thoughtlessness. Now Maria played only light tunes and waltzes in his presence. She practiced the music that satisfied her own taste in front of the portrait of her mother that hung, life-size, over the piano. "You would have been pleased with me," she said to her mother in her thoughts. "You would have known that I only needed to want it in order to become an

3

artist. But I will not want it, I am not allowed to. People like us are not permitted that. Would you also have thought so, Mother?"

Her glance rested with passionate fervor on the noble countenance that so resembled her own. It was the same perfect oval, the same forehead shaded by small curls of thick, ash-blonde hair. Her forehead formed two barely perceptible elevations above the delicate eyebrows and the rather deep-set blue-grey eyes. It was the same cut of the slender nose, the lightly swelling lips, and the same truly regal figure. But a different spirit revealed itself in each of the two beautiful creatures. Maria's entire appearance signaled determination, strength of character, and clarity. The departed one, on the other hand, wore an expression of peculiar melancholy and helpless diffidence. She looked down, eternally young and lovely, from the portrait that had been painted when she was eighteen, in the first year of her marriage. It depicted her in a white lace dress, with her neck bare, her arms hanging carelessly, a white, barely opened rose in her hand. Her head bent slightly forward, she seemed to be listening, lost in a dream. Maria recalled seeing her like that at concerts, at the opera, and also when her father or she spoke to her.

But these happy memories of her mother were long past, and those connected to a later period were unspeakably sad. The countess, overcome by melancholia, had gone into a decline. More and more apathetic, more and more vague, she would wander for hours through the garden in summer, through the rooms and the hallways in winter, would sometimes stand listening at a door, then would make a gesture of horror and, silently and restlessly, resume her wandering.

The first symptoms of this ailment were said to have been caused by a violent shock, whose source no one in Maria's surroundings claimed to know. She did not doubt that a secret was concealed here and was tireless in her attempts to discover it. In particular she besieged with questions her former nanny, who loved her with boundless and slavish devotion.

"Tell me, Lisette, come, tell me," she once pleaded, and, although she was generally miserly with her displays of affection, she put her arm around the neck of the faithful woman. "If you love me, tell me right now, this minute . . . . If you don't tell me, I'll know that I don't mean anything to you."

Lisette's shoulders sagged. Her gray eyes stared helplessly and despairingly into space, her cheeks grew pale, and her lips trembled. "I wish that I were dead," she moaned, "so that the child could no longer ask me."

Dead? Maria stepped away from her and bowed her head.

Lisette had wished her own death. She who could not bear to hear of death, who viewed anyone who mentioned it as her enemy, who prized life as the most precious possession and expected so much from it, who wanted to dance at Maria's wedding and to raise the children of that child, all of them, even if there were twelve of them! Lisette had wished her own death!

The young girl was deeply moved and had to fight back tears in order to say loudly and clearly, "I will never ask you again."

Maria had kept her word. Since then six years had passed.

II.

The curtain of the adjoining room was pushed back gently; Lisette appeared at the entrance and, in her soft, deferential voice, asked, "Maria, child, may I come in?"

"You're still awake?" was the reproachful response, and Lisette apologized, "I had already gone to bed, long ago. But you know that I can't fall asleep until I hear your carriage drive up to the house."

"How ridiculous," Maria replied and turned away and seated herself in an armchair.

Lisette came closer and rested her arm on the back of the chair. "I can't fall asleep before that. And then Klara has to come and report to me — and if she should ever forget to! — 'She is here and cheerful and in good spirits.' But today I heard, 'She looked sad.'"

"That is spying!" Maria interrupted her.

"Call it what you like, it's all the same to me, but just don't think you can change it. So the child is sad? Oh, yes, I see it." Her tone became distressed; a painful anxiety spread over her small, pointed face. "What has happened?"

"Oh, Lisette, please, don't make a fuss. What should have happened to me? I am upset, yes, but for a reason that shouldn't worry you."

"We'll see about that. Tell me, my little bird, tell me, so that I can go to bed reassured."

Maria raised her head and looked firmly and severely into the eyes of the servant who bent down to her. "The people who must spend the night in the cold and who, hungry and freezing, will sweep the streets — I am sorry for them."

Lisette started back with a laugh. "Oh, the child! No, that's really too funny. These people who thank God for the snow He allows to fall so that they may have work, who wish for nothing but work, who have been used to work their whole lives — you pity these people!" She was interrupted in the praises she now began to sing of Maria's "golden angel's heart."

There was a commotion in the courtyard outside the young countess's apartments. A clatter of hoofs could be heard. The porter's bell announced the arrival of the master of the house.

Lisette took her leave, and Maria went to meet her father at the threshold; they greeted one another with a clasp of the hand.

"Good morning and good evening," said Maria. "I wanted to see you for a moment this afternoon, but Walter said you had a visitor."

5

"Dornach was with me and stayed so long that I hardly had time to dress for dinner."

"Where?"

"At Princess Alma's."

"Was it nice?"

"You can imagine how it was. Thirty guests, thirty ranks, and thirty courses."

"You're exaggerating, as you always do when it concerns a party at Alma's. Whatever she does or does not do, you criticize it all. And I know how distressing that is to her and how highly she values your opinion."

With these words, Maria placed a cup of tea before the count, who had seated himself in an armchair next to the table. He cast a strange, almost threatening glance at her but lowered his eyes quickly when he encountered only complete candor in his daughter's expression.

Even now that he was in his late forties, Wolfsberg was still considered a man dangerous to women. He was of medium height, of slender and supple build, a famed rider and huntsman. Thanks to a certain cool and dignified reserve, he had a reputation for great dependability, which won him many friends. Orphaned early, he had — in every sense of the word — enjoyed his education in Germany with relatives of his deceased mother. Gifted with an unusual talent for learning, he had been a good student without exerting any effort, and even later it remained his ambition to represent each of his successes as having been effortlessly achieved.

"I don't take life seriously," he would often say, and his face would assume at the same time an almost grim expression.

But there was one thing in life that he did take seriously, and that was his daughter and the happiness he wanted to assure her in both the present and the future.

"Maria," he began, "someone asked today for permission to visit our house. You can probably guess who it was."

She smiled at him happily. "Felix Tessin."

"Tessin? You are joking."

"That was not my intention," Maria replied and lowered her eyes in confusion.

"What? You believe that I would have listened to Tessin if he had come to me with such an impudent request?"

"Why not?" she asked, hesitating, and her father, clearly intending not to be drawn into a discussion, answered, "You should know what I think of him."

"Yes, quite a lot: an intelligent, talented man, for whom you yourself predict a brilliant future."

"That means that I believe he will probably achieve all he strives for. He is ambitious and clever, pursues high but not unattainable goals, and can reach them all the more easily inasmuch as he has no particular scruples about the means to the end."

"Father!"

"Well?"

"That would be terrible."

He shrugged. "Tessin probably views himself, as do so many nowadays, as one who is 'beyond good and evil.' Such an exceptional man, so fascinating with his dark, Manfred-like good looks,[4] so indulged by women." The count spoke calmly and mockingly, without seeming to observe his daughter in the least, but he read in her agitated expression something that pained and surprised him — he was a little too late with his warning. It would not be a matter of erasing a fleeting impression; it would involve uprooting emotions, causing pain. Resting his elbow on the table and his cheek and forehead in his hand, he continued earnestly. "If Tessin were not a relative" — "of your mother's friend," he wanted to say, but could not utter the words — "of Princess Alma, I would have prevented his being introduced to you. As it is, she has made it difficult enough for me to keep him from my house, except in the case of official receptions, from which I cannot exclude a counselor to the ambassador. The good princess has a weakness for him; she cannot forget that she was the dream of his youth, his first and last ideal love."

"Before her marriage; I've heard about it."

"Before and after. What he would not have given to be in the place of his older cousin, Prince Tessin, who made her his bride. It took a while until he tired of aimless pining and took a more practical approach to life and love. And now his attentions can no longer be flattering to a young girl. She shares them with persons with whom she would certainly rather not have anything in common."

"For instance?" asked Maria in a faint voice, and her father scoffed, "Well, really, I should have more respect for the soirées of the *comtesses*.[5] Young ladies no longer gossip at these events; they are no longer interested in the deeds and misdeeds of young men. Their finest silly escapades are wasted, since they make no impression. What do the young *comtesses* know if they know nothing about Mademoiselle Nicolette, the star of the first quadrille?"

Maria had been very pale, but now her cheeks flushed. "On the contrary — they know a great deal and gossip even more about her and about the count. But I don't listen when aspersions are cast on others — you taught me that." She tried to assume a jesting tone but did not succeed; it was too difficult. She could have wept and sobbed aloud.

The count saw it and was sorry for her, but he did not give way to weak impulses. It had to be; she must overcome this infatuation. Even without the decisive reason that would have to be kept from her, Wolfsberg would never have allowed a marriage between Maria and the dissolute Tessin. He therefore replied, "Evil gossip is sometimes on target."

Maria sighed audibly. "You are perhaps unfair to him," she ventured to object.

"He is untruthful and unscrupulous — don't interrupt me — I am speaking of the sort of unscrupulousness that differs from that of the cheat or the thief, as the intangible differs from the tangible. Enough." He turned suddenly and looked at her. "Your guess was wrong. The one who asked me for the opportunity to become known to you — since he claims to know you already — is Hermann Dornach."

She bit her lip. "What an honor! And what was your response?"

"That I would speak to you and then give him an answer. It will be an affirmative, if you take my wishes into consideration. You do not commit yourself to anything by doing so. I ask only: observe him, examine your heart. He will win your respect, but only liking will decide the matter, and — with that we have reached the limits of our free will. Reason states, and the clear eye sees, that this is a man so excellent that a good woman must be happy with him. It is hardly possible that her friendship and esteem for him could do anything but grow into love and enthusiasm. And then there is another man, at whose side she must expect one disappointment after another. She is warned, almost suspects it herself, but what good does it do? A dark instinct is her master. She is indifferent to what is genuine and feels herself irresistibly drawn to what is false."

"Irresistibly?" Defiance and anger flashed from Maria's eyes. "If you apply that word to me, you don't know me."

"Hoho!" he said, quite pleased with the impression he had produced. "Then I have no choice but to apologize. But I do have one question — were you never laughed at for undertaking to defend Mademoiselle Nicolette and her patron?" He spared her the answer that she, with difficulty, attempted to give. "Also, why did you say 'What an honor!' when I delivered Dornach's message?"

"Because the entire world would see it that way. It's quite incredible how they carry on with him. The papas and mamas pay court to the young man — oh, if they could literally throw their daughters at him, one would see *comtesses* flying! And they in turn surpass even their parents in their tactlessness toward him and toward his alter ego, his mother. I'm ashamed for them. It's all so disgraceful and for Dornach so humiliating, because it's so impersonal and is only directed at his position and his wealth."

She grew agitated and spoke with a vehemence that was out of proportion to the ostensible cause.

Disconcerted, the count changed the subject and returned only later to the topic of the suitor who, he had decided once and for all, was to become his son-in-law.

After he had left her, Maria went to bed and for the first time in her life could not fall asleep immediately. Each word her father had said about Tessin reverberated painfully in her mind. The memory of all that she had labeled foolish gossip and that she had refused to acknowledge came to life. Now she knew that those she had accused of slander had been right and that her father was right and that she alone had been mistaken in her foolish, blissful faith, in her misplaced admiration of Tessin, in her pride in his chivalrous courtship of her. Good God, that had been as impersonal as the attentions bestowed on Count Dornach. An ambitious diplomat, a practical man, had wished to become the son-in-law of Count Wolfsberg and had taken the requisite steps with charming agility . . . . His heart was not a part of the transaction — it was not even available to be given, since it was already the possession of another.

A torrent of new sensations engulfed Maria. She was the prey of something strange and ugly from which she wanted to free herself, and she could exercise her will — her father would see that, her father as well as someone else . . . .

Her eyelids grew heavy and closed. A moment of stupor, and then she started awake. Did she know now what it meant to hate? No, no . . . . She felt only a deep regret, as though something magnificent and beautiful she had adored had been disfigured. He whom she had placed above all others was untruthful and unscrupulous?

She heard the clock of the nearest church steeple strike two, and then she fell asleep and dreamed that Tessin stepped up to her bed dressed as a snow shoveler, presented his broom to her, and asked her to dance the cotillion. She followed him through the ballroom and was ashamed of her nightgown and her bare feet. She was ashamed as well of her dance partner, who grinned continually and was the real snow shoveler. And as she looked at him, she discovered something peculiar. The ragged man reminded her of her father; he had the same broad forehead, the same thick eyebrows that grew together. Maria bent toward him and said, "At first glance, I noticed something about you — I just didn't know what it was . . . ." She awoke smiling over this dream and with an unbelievably light heart for a young girl whose first illusions had just been destroyed. "It's over," she thought. "I would never have believed that one could recover so quickly from something that certainly seemed like affection. No, it did not only seem like it! The others want me to deceive them, but why should I deceive myself? I loved him, ardently and sincerely."

And, sobbing aloud, she pressed her tear-streaked face into her pillow.

III.

The next day Hermann Dornach paid his first visit, was invited to dinner for the following day, and spent several evenings with the family. Countess Dolph found him charming and unbelievably clever for the heir to a country estate. She valued highly the fact that he was comfortable with her so quickly although she was known for her sharp tongue, which intimidated most people. "It's simply the result of his clear conscience," she declared. "Any accusation against him would be a shot in the dark. He can watch calmly as I sharpen my arrows; he's not among those who dread me."

And in fact, in her presence his gentle bashfulness disappeared — a bashfulness that seemed, to the less experienced, misplaced in a man whom all were eager to indulge, and that was, for those versed in the ways of the heart, the proof of true nobility of soul.

It was said that this shyness was the consequence of the excessive rigidity with which his mother had directed his upbringing. The countess had wanted to administer an antidote both to the obsequiousness of the parasites, the armies of officials, and the servants, and to the boundless indulgence of a weak and ailing father toward his only child. But the dose had been too strong and had prevented not only self-importance, but self-confidence as well. The countess saw the mistake she had made and in time attempted to correct it. After the death of the count, she formally assumed the guardianship of Hermann that she had in fact always exercised, and she now allowed the eighteen-year-old youth unlimited freedom. Some small abuse of the mother's indulgence would have been easily forgiven, but it never occurred. Hermann attended agricultural schools in Germany and England, hunted lions in Nubia and elephants in India, served for several years in an exclusive cavalry regiment, and devoted himself later to the management of his estates. He had reached the age of thirty-three without ever having been in the position of paying debts other than those of his friends, without having seduced a young girl, without having endangered the reputation of a woman. And yet the blood in his veins was as hot as that of any young man of his age or station, and he had, in his few love affairs, expended more true and genuine emotion than all the others in their countless affairs with women from the circus and demi-monde. Since meeting Maria, however, even his most serious former infatuations and passions seemed to him mere trifles.

It happened at a ball, which he had attended only in obedience to his mother's wishes. Indeed, it was only in obedience to her that he came to Vienna at all, in order to enter into a society that gave him no pleasure and where the efforts to court his favor disgusted him.

Aunt Dolph had been witness to his first encounter with Maria and then had herself become the object of his most zealous and respectful attentions. She suddenly remembered her youthful friendship with Countess Agathe Dornach and paid her a visit that was soon returned. The elderly ladies called each other "dear girl," and each felt herself superior to the other, the former close acquaintance from whom dramatically opposing views and an equally brusque intolerance had eventually separated her. Agathe prided herself on being an orthodox Catholic; Dolph, completely irreligious, would not admit that a reasonable person could be pious, unless he were a servant, a peasant, or a prince. Agathe feared for Dolph's eternal salvation, while the latter feared Agathe's attempts to convert her, which always culminated in the assertion that skepticism was the result of inadequate education and that women would not achieve more than

that. Whether these contrasts between the two ladies had been moderated or in-
tensified over the years went uninvestigated, and sensitive subjects were carefully avoided. The count, a peerless conversationalist, helped them easily
through a few evenings; the conversation he dominated was more lively than
that between the two young people at the tea table next to them. Maria was silent; Hermann not talkative. He nevertheless said a great deal, for his every
glance held a passionate declaration of the most ardent love.

One day, then, Countess Agathe was announced to Maria and entered with
the air of having come to deliver the key to heaven. With dignified composure,
she presented on Hermann's behalf the request that he be allowed to ask for
Maria's hand.

"Your consent would make him very happy," she concluded, "and you can
give it to him without hesitation. I flatter no one, least of all myself in my son.
My opinion of him is that of every impartial observer — there is no one better,
more sensible, or more noble." She paused and waited for a response; as none
followed, she continued, "If your mother were still alive, I would have turned
first to her and she would have been the one to speak to you now. Imagine that
she is speaking to you through me."

Maria lowered her eyes; her lips trembled, but she was silent.

"Certain happiness is seldom offered to us in life. It is unlikely to return to
one who has refused it once." The countess resumed her speech after a brief
pause, this time more coldly and more formally. "Still, you are right to reflect.
Your hesitation pleases me; it proves that you recognize the seriousness of the
step that other young girls take rashly. I have confidence in you. If I may take
home with me your assent, your simple assent, it will embody for me all the ho-
liest vows that an honest girl could ever make to her future husband."

"Yes, it would embody those . . . . I beg of you, Countess Dornach — "

"What? Countess Dornach? Am I still a stranger to you?"

"I beg of you, dear Agathe, tell Count Hermann" — an unspeakable anxiety
overcame her; she studied the countess's marble features. "As cold as my aunt,"
she thought.

"Well, what shall I tell him?"

"That this evening — you're both coming, aren't you? — I will speak to
him myself."

She kissed the hand of the countess, who rose looking quite disappointed,
and accompanied her to the stairs.

Back in her room, she paced for a long time in great agitation and tormented
herself with the question, "Why do I want to do it? Is my motivation not repre-
hensible?" And then she seated herself at the piano and played and became
gradually more composed. And then Aunt Dolph came and read her a telegram
from Wilhelm Dornach, an acquaintance from the distant past, whose existence
she had long since forgotten. Based on a rumor that had penetrated even into his

rural isolation, the good, foolish fellow sent his best wishes on the occasion of her niece's engagement to his cousin.

The countess laughed at the poor devil's haste to feign his joy. As the second in line to inherit the estate, the man, completely without property and cursed with a large family, could hardly have wished anything but that his cousin remain single. An indiscreet wish, of course, but the most natural thing in the world. She took a seat on the couch with her back to the portrait of her deceased sister-in-law, which she generally avoided looking at, complained of a headache, and rubbed her sunken temples with cologne. She was ill and irritable. Even when she took up her current favorite topic, praising Hermann, her praise was mixed with mockery.

"Happy the woman he marries," she cried. "Her marriage will be peaceful, like all those where *one* will prevails."

She answered Maria's astonished expression with a question: had not Hermann learned, from childhood on, to submit himself to a petticoat government? How foolish a woman would be if she did not know how to use those splendid early lessons as the basis for further education! Good instructions on how best to begin followed now in profusion — the serious as well as the facetious, and all of it illustrated by examples. Take the Heinbergs. At first he was a gambler and spent his nights at the casino, while she stayed at home and cried. That changed little by little — thanks to her! Now *she* gambles and *he* cries. "And your friend Emmy, who let herself be dragged to the altar like a lamb to the slaughter and who found in her marriage a good, safe haven, from which she can embark on all sorts of adventurous journeys out into the stormy sea!"

A knock at the door was heard, and Miss Ninnemann, Countess Dolph's lady companion, slipped into the room. Her mistress called her "Ninny," which roused her indignation, and, as a result of the agitation that accompanied her employment, she suffered from nervousness. Although she now had only an innocuous message to deliver — that the dressmaker had come and had said she could not wait long — her mouth twitched convulsively as she did it.

"Very well, sit down," Dolph replied and continued censuring friend and foe alike. She mentioned many names only casually and in passing; nevertheless, the bearer of the name then seemed sullied or ridiculous.

Maria listened to her today more attentively than usual and thought, "She is probably right. What good could there be in others if Tessin is worthless?" And Countess Dolph, like a true actor, who is inspired by the attention of even a single spectator, outdid herself in her questionable art and worked herself into that intoxication of wit and maliciousness that agreed with her so well. Her face, which, as she said herself, was a caricature of her brother's, became animated, and her headache disappeared.

Miss Ninnemann finally lost her patience and rose, her complexion even a shade redder than usual. "I will tell the dressmaker," she said, "that the countess is busy slandering right now and has no time for her."

Dolph laughed. "Ha! My slandering is an honest fellow who lays his cards on the table. But yours! When you begin, 'I like him or her quite a lot,' it's like a rider who pulls up his horse before giving him a cut with the whip."

She left in the highest of spirits and was cheerful at dinner later and apparently feeling quite well. In the evening, however, her headache suddenly reappeared and forced the sufferer to retire to her room shortly before Hermann and his mother were announced. Uncustomarily, Wolfsberg had dined at home and had kept the ladies company in the drawing room that afternoon. He received the countess with the thousand apologies of his sister, who had most inopportunely become ill; Agathe expressed her sympathy with particular warmth and entreated the count to take her to her friend, which he did at once.

The young people were left alone.

Both blushed. To him it seemed that the opportunity for a decisive conversation had been offered in a tactless and awkward manner; she, on the other hand, was overcome by painful emotion, half indignation, half dread. She stood there motionless, her brows drawn together, looking into the light of the fire. After a pause that was more difficult to end the longer it lasted, Hermann began, agitated and hesitating.

"My mother spoke with you, Countess — you know the audacious question that I have presumed to put to you. The slightest hope of an affirmative answer would make me very happy . . . . Will you give me that hope?"

Maria remained silent, but she turned a bit and looked askance at him, in a manner so distant that it was as though she were seeing him today for the first time. His appearance was extraordinarily winning, she had to admit. Intelligence, kindness, frankness expressed themselves in his handsome face, radiated from his honest eyes. He had a small moustache and side-whiskers, his thick brown hair was cut short and revealed his nobly formed forehead and his temples. His figure had something solid and strong about it, and yet it did not lack masculine grace.

"Answer me," he said.

And she, "the hero" in her circle of young friends, the intrepid one, who had made up her mind and was firmly resolved to place her hand in that of the suitor she did not love, now whispered in dismay, "I don't know . . . I don't know . . . ."

Her despair moved and touched him; he reproached himself — he had asked too soon; he should not have given way to the urging of his mother, should not have allowed himself to be led by the count's willingness to oblige. Now he endeavored to make amends for his haste. "You are still undecided," he began again. "I see that and find it understandable. Think it over, examine me critically and at length. I will not make it difficult for you — there are no unfathomable depths in my soul."

"My God, no," said Maria, "that is not — no, no . . . ." And two words, the extent of her youthful wisdom, fell almost inaudibly from her lips . . . the words of her father, which he had impressed upon his willing pupil: "Stay calm!" Long ago, when she had thrown herself in despair over the body of her dead mother . . . . And much later, while hunting, when her horse had shied and raced toward the millstream . . . . And then at her first ball, when she, seized by high-spirited gaiety, had laughed so loudly, danced so wildly . . . . His forceful "Stay calm!" had always brought her to her senses.

At this moment, too, her recollection of her father's admonition was not in vain, and she was able to add, with some appearance of composure, to her incoherent words, "You are mistaken — I have decided."

"To do what? No!"

"Yes."

"Blessed fortune!" he cried, with the deepest exultation, and seized her hand, which she, again overcome by her earlier anxiety, attempted to free from his. He, however, held it fast.

"It is mine, my most precious possession — and you give it freely, Maria, don't you? No one has influenced you — you would not have allowed yourself to be influenced; you are too proud, too independent."

"On the contrary," she replied and lifted her bowed head at last. Never in her life had she seen someone so moved, and — strangely — what she had considered to be the embodiment of ridiculousness, a lover whose sentiments are not completely returned, now seemed to her to be very serious and even sad — sad for her. He, with his great and genuine emotion, he was the rich one, and she was poor in comparison. "On the contrary," she repeated softly, "my father's wish did influence me — at first."

"And later, what decided you later, what decides you now? Be honest with me, Countess, as I will always be with you. What decides you . . . I — I know that it is not affection." He uttered this admission with difficulty, for he did not deceive himself as to the danger that it involved.

But Maria smiled, almost joyfully. "That you nevertheless want to take a chance on me, that is what decides me . . . . And the confidence that you demonstrate to me — and the confidence that you inspire in me."

"Thank you!" he said, and a blissful conviction shone in his honest blue eyes. "That is a splendid alliance: your confidence and my reverent love. A love such as mine will suffice for two good hearts; it has a communicative power. Do you know why? Because it never forces itself upon others, never feels entitled to privilege. There is no duty it requires, only favor and benevolence. And what noble woman's soul would not finally be touched by . . . . Enough!" He stopped himself. "Otherwise I will yet reveal that this magnanimity is nothing but the greatest selfishness — the selfish desire to see you happy."

With both hands he drew her hand to his lips, to his breast. Maria felt the tumultuous beating of his heart, but his face, which bent over hers, was peaceful, and it seemed to her as though transfigured by the most profound bliss.

The silent man grew eloquent. He found engaging expression for his sentiments, persuasive words for his thoughts. Maria listened to him and thought,
"He is true and warm." And perhaps that was what she had longed for since
childhood: truth and warmth. Certainly she had been idolized and indulged, but
how much insincerity had there been in the idolatry proffered her by the servile, how much — at least external — coldness in the indulgence she had experienced from her father and now from Aunt Dolph.

"The seriousness of your brow bewitched me; that is what I first loved about
you, and now my ardent desire will be to banish it little by little. You shall travel
safe and sound through life, enveloped in my love . . . . I am too happy," he
burst out, "I do not deserve it — what must he be who would deserve you,
Maria! Maria!"

She took a step back. She avoided the glance that, filled with passionate devotion, sought hers, and said, "No, not like that — you are better than I am . . .
be patient with me."

IV.

They became a quiet and solemn betrothed couple. Maria remained cool and
sedate. Dornach successfully fought against every stirring of his overflowing
emotion. Disagreements arose in society, because some insisted that it was *she*
who was more indifferent to *him* and others were certain that *he* was more indifferent to *her*. Nevertheless, all the world launched into such enthusiastic and
heartfelt congratulations that one might have thought Romeo and Juliet had
risen from their graves and were about to set up housekeeping.

Among the many superficial people, whose empty chatter had to be endured
and who had to be thanked for their curiosity, which masqueraded as solicitude,
there were nevertheless a few devoted, kindly ones as well, especially Princess
Alma Tessin. Maria loved her, honored her infinitely kind heart, and was full of
compassion for her timidity, which increased from year to year. The princess
sought Maria's advice, kissed her hands, and had in her presence something
humble and shamefaced about her, which virtually forced upon Maria a superiority over the woman who could almost have been her mother.

One morning Princess Tessin came to see Aunt Dolph and found the couple
there. Maria went to meet her; Hermann rose. She saw him for the first time
since his engagement, and it occurred unexpectedly. Her delicate complexion
changed color.

"Count Dornach," she said, "I have not yet had the opportunity to give you
my sincere, my happy — " She stopped, overcome by an insurmountable confusion, and looked beseechingly up at him. "Have mercy," she seemed to say. "See
what I am suffering and have mercy." Her mute plea went unanswered. He
bowed, murmured a few polite phrases, and did not take the hand that she,
trembling, had stretched toward him and now let fall with a gesture of despair.

Hermann bade them farewell and left.

Dissatisfaction with him filled Maria's heart. What right did he have to behave so negatively toward someone so dear to her? It flashed through her mind — Alma was related to Tessin. But no — neither Dornach nor anyone else could have any idea of the fleeting interest which that man had inspired in her. Tessin had ostensibly not paid her more attention than twenty others. That she had felt a preference for him remained her own closely guarded secret, even from him. But jealousy has sharp eyes — perhaps it made the unsuspecting Hermann clairvoyant.

When he returned in the evening, bringing one of the lovely bouquets with him that arrived daily from the greenhouses of Dornach for its future mistress, Maria refused to accept the gift.

"First I want to know what you have against Alma."

He hesitated with his answer. "She is . . . honesty above all, don't you think? . . . Well, then — I find her unpleasant."

"Unpleasant? Excuse me, but I can't understand that — unless you have discovered the art of loathing beauty and kindness," she exclaimed acidly, and he responded with his customary even temper, "I said nothing of loathing Princess Tessin; I admire her beauty . . . ."

"She looks exactly as she is," Maria interjected with feeling. "So blond, so fair, so delicate, bathed in an otherworldly grace — in my childhood I imagined that angels were like that."

These words made a strange impression on him; a shadow of embarrassment crossed his face, and at the same time the deepest and most tender compassion was reflected therein.

"I will cure you of your aversion," Maria continued. "The remedy is simple: you must become better acquainted with Alma, and then my best friend will become yours as well and will find a second home with us — if that is all right with you."

He found it difficult to suppress the joy that the words "with us" aroused in him, but he restrained himself and answered, "You shall receive whomever you like in your house, and you shall do whatever you please; it will be all right with me. Will you take the flowers now?"

"With pleasure, and thank you," she answered, thinking, "He is a splendid person, and I will love him like a brother."

Dornach continued to show his devotion in the most unassuming manner. The inventive attentions he paid to his bride were in his eyes a matter of course; a sign of her approval or a cheerful glance was to him a gift from heaven. Countess Dolph teased him and assured him that he put the knights of the round table to shame; such an old-fashioned chivalrous lover would find life as a husband difficult.

Hermann laughed and declared that he neither did nor wished to do anything other than what was proper. That Maria had confided to him her motto "Stay calm!" and that he abided by his: "Do what's proper."

And so his lavish gifts, and the unprecedented generosity of his marriage settlement, and every evidence of his boundless solicitude for the present and future comfort and well-being of his bride were "the proper thing."

Countess Dornach conducted herself with respect to her son's fiancée just as he did; his conduct had suddenly become her guide. To this woman, governed as she was by an orthodox sense of family tradition, the young bachelor Hermann had been transformed into the future head of his noble family, worthy of respect, and it befitted the older generation to — make way. With magnificent equanimity, Agathe gave precedence to the woman who would now take her place as the first lady of Dornach. She renounced the family jewelry in favor of Maria with as much indifference as if it had been a pair of worn gloves. She made arrangements to move out of the palace into a rented apartment in the city, where she planned to spend several of the winter months, and to the widow's estate, Dornachtal,[6] where she wished to spend most of the year. The latter was a gloomy house in the bleak countryside at the foot of the Braneker mountains, and Hermann tried everything possible to dissuade his mother from the move. She should stay in Dornach in the wing of the castle that she had always preferred to the other three. There she had enjoyed her brief marital bliss, there she had lived for a generation as mistress of the house, there she should continue living in proximity to her children, honored, loved, but undisturbed by them. She would not allow herself to be swayed; her resolve was unwavering. She thanked God, she said, for finally granting her the opportunity to spend the last years of her life in peace and in prayer for herself and her loved ones.

Although everything the countess said and did was irreproachable, Maria was unable to feel real affection for her; this irreproachability was practiced too frostily. Her father's reserved manner inspired her admiration because she assumed that it concealed great riches. The countess's reserve, on the other hand, seemed to her to mask a deficiency. When she took her leave at the end of a visit to her fiancé's mother, she received a kiss on the forehead; its icy coldness made her shiver from head to toe.

Once, when Countess Dornach had wanted to give her a new demonstration of her immense capacity for renunciation, Maria ventured to resist. Agathe smiled, lifted her regal chin, and said, "Don't take it too seriously, dear child — perhaps I am only doing it for Countess Dornach."

On the evening before the wedding, Count Wolfsberg sent for his daughter. He waited for her, seated at his desk in his large armchair, his head back, his legs crossed, and reflected on what he wanted to say to her. There was much to say. That she had been a good and obedient child to him, had never caused him a moment's unhappiness, that the farewell would be difficult for him, but that he would take comfort in the constant hope that she would be happy. And then praise of Hermann and some good advice for the future. To the count it was a certainty, confirmed by a hundred examples, that every innocent young woman falls in love with the man who is the first to teach her about life. Maria will be no exception, and he wanted to enjoin her not to become selfish in her passion and always to maintain her dignity. The fidelity that a man vows to his wife at the altar, he believed, was different from the fidelity she vows to him. A husband's apparent neglect, a fleeting amusement will be overlooked by the woman who respects herself. What is a brief moment of sensuality, usually followed by miserable disenchantment, in comparison to the unwavering, grateful attachment to the revered life's companion who never requires consideration but always shows it . . . or should — and woe unto her if she did not, if she, like the poor woman he had once adored . . . .

The count sighed deeply; his countenance darkened. The most painful memory of his life had awakened within him, and he did not seek, as he usually did, to escape it. A sweet figure rose before him: the love of his youth, his hard-won wife. Count Wolfsberg was not a suitor of equal birth for a daughter of the family from which she was descended; they entered into royal alliances or they remained unmarried. And nevertheless he had made her his bride, despite the prejudice against him, because he had known how to win her passionate heart, because she, forced to renounce him, would have died, and because her parents, weak and foolish as they were, did not want to let her die . . . . If they had only permitted that — what a sweet and lovely death would have been hers! She could have left this world with her illusions intact, believing devoutly in her lover. But that was not granted her. She had to learn the worst before she was allowed to depart, had to learn to doubt him, his honesty, his integrity, and his loyalty, everything on which a man's worth is founded. An awful emotion possessed her; she thought it was contempt, but it was jealousy. She herself then dissembled, pretended to suspect nothing, watched and observed him and their guest, his accomplice and victim, the little serpent Alma, who, barely out of the nursery, had just entered into — an admittedly wretched — marriage . . . . She watched and observed and had only one desire, one thought, one goal — to unmask the guilty ones, to hurl the words "Cowards and traitors!" at them. So she stooped to eavesdropping at doors; so she listened and so she heard what robbed her of her sanity.

Her restless and wretched wandering began; she glided through the silent house with light steps whose almost inaudible sound awakened a gnawing, incessant reproach. Years later it came back to the man as he mused, and it aroused, if not remorse, then at least not the indignation he had once felt.

Voices were heard in the next room. Maria exchanged a few words with the valet, who would not have deprived himself of the opportunity to open the door for her today with particular assiduity. She entered and went slowly to her father.

18

"You sent for me. It was unnecessary; I would have come in any case. I still have much to say to you."

He smiled. "Just as I to you. Take a seat."

Maria pushed a chair close to the desk and sat down.

The count glanced at her and then looked obstinately past her at nothing. "The image of her mother," he thought, "but her fate will be a different one. Within the beautiful exterior dwells a stronger soul, a more powerful spirit. She is my child, my dear child, whom I now relinquish . . . ." A sudden melancholy overcame him, a sort of pity for himself, which he mocked. Was he perhaps beginning to get old and sentimental? He pulled himself together and sat upright. "Tomorrow, then — "

"Tomorrow, then, Father — " A tremor ran through her entire body; she bent over and, not heeding his defensive gesture, fell to her knees before him and threw her arms around his neck. "Just once let me thank you," she said in a choked voice. "Just once let me say: I thank you for everything."

A dry sob burst from him. He pressed her to him so tightly that she could hardly breathe, he pressed his lips to her hair, to her forehead, and clasped her again and again to his breast.

Finally both rose and paced up and down together for a long time in earnest conversation.

It was past midnight when the count sent his daughter away with a short "Good night, Maria." She was already standing at the door when he called her back. He felt moved to give her a last gift, a memento of this hour. Searching, he looked about the room; his glance rested upon a costly, gold-inlaid box, which stood on a cabinet. "Take this, it has long been yours; it belonged to your poor mother."

V.

At the wedding the next day everything was exemplary: the organization of it all, the behavior of the bridal couple, the attire of the bride, the arrival at the church, the ceremony, the banquet, and Dornach's carriage, which brought the young newlyweds to the north train station in the evening. They had chosen a slow train in order not to arrive too early in the morning at the castle, where a ceremonial reception awaited them.

Maria pressed herself into a corner of the compartment. A shiver of fear had rippled through her as the door was closed. Now she was alone with the man who loved her and who had legal dominion over her. Only yesterday she had felt herself stronger than he; how suddenly that had changed — now she trembled before him.

He noticed it, and his heart swelled with pride and happiness. "Do not be afraid," he would have liked to cry out to her. "You are as sacred to me as you are dear. Neither your father nor the priest could give you to me — you alone

19

can do that, and I will work and strive for this most precious possession." But he thought, no, not words, but proof! And then he spoke of all sorts of things, but not of anything profound. Of the weather, which would hopefully be as lovely tomorrow as it — what astonishing constancy for April! — had been the whole week. How that made him happy, because Dornach would show itself to its mistress for the first time in sunshine, which it certainly needed in order not to make too gloomy an impression. He arranged pillows and blankets and invited Maria to make herself comfortable and to rest for a few hours; she must be tired and tomorrow would be another strenuous day. Maria acceded willingly to his request; she wanted at least to pretend to sleep, even though sleep was impossible, thanks to the uncanny sensation that filled her in the presence of this man — her husband. Now and then she opened her eyes a little and looked over at him and encountered each time the infinitely loving gaze he directed at her. There was something about it that gradually made her feel safe; her anxiety disappeared; her eyelids grew heavy and closed. What she had thought was impossible occurred: she fell into a deep, sound sleep.

The sun had been up an hour when Maria awoke with a start. Hermann was standing at the window and greeted her with a cheerful "Good morning!" that she returned with great embarrassment. Her eyes shone like those of a child just waking, her cheeks were flushed — how well the early morning light and her youthful beauty agreed with one another!

Hermann took her by the hand and led her to the window. "Do you see the blue mountain range there?" he said. "Its outlines melt into the dazzling colors of the horizon. In front of it, quite under its protection, there is a row of hills. Do you see them?"

"Oh, yes, and the contrast between the dark background of the mountains and the cheerful hills is pretty."

"On one of them there's a gray stone edifice. That's Castle Dornach. I had always liked it exceedingly, but recently, on my last visit, when I thought of it as your future home, it seemed quite unworthy of you, old owl's nest that it is."

Maria protested not only out of politeness; the view of the manor house, now hidden from her by a turn in the road, had seemed magnificent to her.

They rolled on through meadows along the bank of a swift stream toward the station where they left the train. The trip continued by carriage to the first forester's house in Dornach's territory, where Maria would be able to rest undisturbed and where she was awaited only by the servants she had sent on ahead. Lisette had put herself in charge and, with her hostile mood, had brought them all to the brink of despair. For several weeks she had been in the castle supervising the furnishing of Maria's quarters. And now she had come here, because she of course must be the first to greet the poor child who had been snatched from her care. She did so in a flood of tears and with outbursts of regret, as though they had been separated for years; toward Hermann, on the other hand, she wrapped herself in venomous silence. He stifled a laugh, offered his wife his

20

arm, and led her, once she had gently extricated herself from her worshipper and tyrant, into the house.

Lisette rushed after them and was disappointed anew. The mistress did not speak a word of complaint or accusation as she changed her clothes. Lisette had counted on such a complaint in order to open the floodgates to the animosity, dammed up in her since yesterday, toward the roughness and the impertinence of new husbands. She was quite put out that she was offered no opportunity of relief. Maria was cheerful and remained so during the entire drive, which at her request was soon resumed. Lisette and the chambermaid followed close upon the master and mistress's carriage and four. The former rose often from her seat, put on her glasses, and studied, as much as it was possible, her idol's face. It seemed to her that the ill-bred child looked absolutely enthusiastic when they reached the edge of the village of Dornach and the inhabitants gave their new fellow citizen a ceremonial reception. It did not differ in its program from all the other ceremonial receptions that take place in the good land of Moravia: triumphal arches, speeches, gifts of bread and salt, eggs, chickens, ducks, geese, a gigantic baby made of gingerbread in colorful clothing and a trimmed bonnet, gun salutes, and cries of "Hurrah!" What was unusual, however, was the genuine affection that animated the proclamations, ennobled the awkward, and stamped the customary with something of the new and exceptional.

"You are well loved by these people," Maria said to Hermann.

"Because I love *them*," he said, with pleasure. "If there is anything on earth that we are repaid with interest and compound interest, it is our love for others. To go through life unloved is more than misfortune; it is one's own fault."

In the village square, a large crowd surrounded the entrance to the church. Under the portal stood the aged dean with his chaplains and the choirboys swinging censers. As the count and countess left the carriage in order to enter the house of God, the jubilant shouts of the throng died away; the bronze voices of the bells now spoke alone and accompanied with their ringing the blessing that the elderly priest invoked from heaven for the young couple.

They emerged from the church; they descended the wide steps slowly. All eyes were on Maria, with open curiosity, with shyness, with astonished admiration — in the eyes of many a youth glowed obvious rapture . . . . Whether young or old, whether female or male, on all the faces turned to her Maria read the expression of a mysterious, inherited suffering. And a thought awakened within her: "What calls to you here with mute and unconscious lamentation is eternal servitude striving for deliverance. We the masters, they the bondsmen. Impoverished in body and soul, they earn — our bread; they labor, bent to the ground, year in, year out, in order that our intellect may fly free and unhindered to the limits of knowledge . . . . Without their hard work, there would be no rest for us, no pleasure, neither art nor science . . . ."

Having reached the foot of the steps, she stopped suddenly and reached, as though involuntarily seeking protection, for Hermann's arm. He clasped her to him and lifted her into the coach, where he asked, full of concern, about the reason for her sudden alarm.

"It's nothing," she assured him. "Nothing at all."

And it really was nothing — an illusion, an odd trick her memory had played on her. She had thought she had seen, in the middle of the milling crowd, someone laughing mockingly at her, someone who stared at her as insolently as on that winter night. Features so repugnant because they mirrored those of a revered countenance in such a distorted manner. "Nonsense," she said to herself. "How could he be here?"

The distressing impression had vanished, driven away by many beautiful and charming ones and by a vigorous lightheartedness that flooded through her entire being as she flew onward with the quick trot of the fiery, frothing horses over the velvety soft road that ascended through majestic beeches. Every glimpse of the countryside allowed by the low-hanging branches met with a lovely view. The landscape, with its meadows and clusters of trees resplendent in the first green of spring, with its ponds and diligently rushing streams, resembled a well-kept park.

And now one saw a pointed roof and richly ornamented chimneys and gables towering among high treetops. Finally they reached the avenue as well, and there stood Castle Dornach, gray with age, magnificent. It had been built at the time of Pierre Nepveu[7] (by Nepveu himself, according to legend) in a mixture of Gothic and Renaissance styles: a proud monument to power established long ago and maintained through the centuries.

With the eye of a connoisseur, Maria examined the picturesque structure; her artistic sense of beauty luxuriated in utmost gratification. Such surroundings are bliss — bliss every hour of the day. How often had she, as a young girl, restored in her mind the ruins her father had allowed to fall into disrepair in the forest of Wolfsberg, embellishing them with towers and sculpture and graceful bay windows, until the creation of her imagination became almost as splendid as the reality she saw now before her.

"My dream," she cried, "my dream realized and surpassed!"

The broad gravel path in front of the house swarmed with a crowd calling its welcome.

"The last onslaught," Hermann said, "the officials and the foresters."

"All right," she replied. "But, tell me, who receives the first handshake? The giant with the blond mane at the head of the army — am I right?" She indicated a tall, broad-shouldered man with a reddish brown face and fair hair, who wore a dress-coat that was too tight and a necktie that was too loose. On his right stood a stately brown-eyed lady; on his left were arranged organ-pipes come to life: eight boys, the oldest of whom was tall enough to reach his elbow, the youngest the leg of his boots, and who all had the same fair hair as he.

Hermann waved at him from afar. "Yes, he receives the first handshake, he, my excellent cousin Wilhelm."

The cousin nodded and bowed and in a gruff tone ordered his boys to do likewise, and his spouse did so unbidden.

Radiantly happy, hand in hand with Maria, Hermann now stepped before the group. "Here she is," he cried. "I've brought her — " and turning to the rest of the assemblage, "here she is, your mistress and mine."

Good heavens, what had the count done with that precipitous introduction! Not more and not less than thrown the well-prepared, doggedly rehearsed greeting ceremony into irreparable confusion. One or two cheers rang out, joined by far too few voices.

"*You* should have started," the commander of the fire brigade snapped at the commander of the veterans.

"Why me? When the carriage stops, I was told. Did it stop? The master and mistress jumped out while it was still rolling. But no matter — fire! Fire, I say — confound it!"

A volley was fired, banners waved.

"'Your Grace' — ," whispered the director to Count Wilhelm.

"'His Lordship,'" said the steward.

"'Your Lordship,'" corrected the secretary.

But Cousin Wilhelm, shaken to the depths of his manly soul, could not remember a single word of the stirring speech that the schoolmaster had written for him and impressed on his memory so well, so firmly, that he had just a moment ago said, full of pride, "Helmi, Master, it's all inside; it's as solid as iron."

And now suddenly everything was gone.

The hellish work of memorization had been for naught, as were the poor author's mortal terror and intoxicating hopes; the good countess's unassuming pleasure was shattered. She had hoped to witness her husband in an oratorical triumph like the one he had recently enjoyed at the local shooting range. At this most important moment there was nothing but a twitch beneath his thick moustache and over his round, smooth-shaven cheeks, and his eyes, which were small rather than large and nevertheless contained an ocean, a dark blue ocean of love, traveled from Hermann to Maria and from Maria to Hermann. Suddenly he cried, "Hermann, old boy! Your Ladyship, most esteemed cousin — you are heartily welcome. Away!" he snapped at the teacher, who had drawn nearer in order to prompt him, and the village band started up, trumpeting, fiddling, and drumming.

Hermann embraced his cousin, kissed the hand of Countess Helmi, and gave the boys a sign that they should present the bouquets they had been holding in readiness for their new aunt. All of them rushed toward her and all of them, from the four-year-old to the fourteen-year-old, had the same face, and each was as open and as trusting as the next. And why not? Were they not looking their best, were they not handsome in their new linen shirts, sewn by their mother, and with faces freshly washed by their mother and teeth brushed today with toothpowder?

Maria was as friendly to the whole family as a perfectly elegant young lady can possibly be to the most pronounced sort of rustic gentry. She charmed the husband and wife, she charmed everyone who was introduced to her and with whom she exchanged a few words. Her simple and tactful good nature won her universal affection in the first hour and conquered the prejudices of the elderly chief officials, who had anticipated the new regime with misgiving.

In a thoroughly pleasant mood, the "old guard," as the higher officials were called by the cheery wife of a younger colleague, returned home late in the evening after the dinner at the manor. Gentlemen and ladies alike were in complete agreement that the young countess was inexpressibly gracious and simply — a lady.

"Every inch a lady!" cried the well-bred secretary. "And — such dignity, such refinement . . . . You understand me, madam," he said to the steward's wife.

As he was saying good-bye to his relatives, Hermann asked, "When will you come again? Tomorrow?"

Wilhelm started back, as though a shameful wrong had been demanded of him. "What are you thinking of? In a week at the earliest. Isn't that right, Helmi?"

"Not for the world would we come earlier," she replied. "That is, in any case, tactless enough."

"All right, a week from today. Agreed!"

"Agreed. Of course we'll come without the scamps . . . . Will you be quiet?" he blustered at his firstborn, who had permitted himself to grumble at this paternal decree. "The scamps will stay home, the scamps have to study, have to learn everything I didn't learn, and that's a lot."

He picked up Hansel, the youngest, who had long since fallen asleep on a sofa, and followed his wife, whom the master of the house escorted to the carriage, and his other sons, who had marched on ahead.

At the door, to which Maria had accompanied him, he stopped, looked into her eyes, and, resting his cheek on the child's head, said, "The eighth! It's a number — sometimes I'm embarrassed — actually, I'm embarrassed each time in retrospect and in advance, because — who knows — and who can know — what is still to come? But — " and here his heart overflowed; he had not counted how many times that had happened this evening, "even if twice as many more come along as are already here, each will grow into a fine human being and a loyal friend, Countess — that is, cousin — to your future sons, the first of whom may you bestow on us as soon as possible."

VI.

"You have given me in marriage to a good and noble man," Maria wrote to her father in her first letter from Dornach. The word "happiness" did not appear in it, but every line expressed contentment. Maria had realized very soon that she, as Hermann's wife, would have a mission to fulfill that suited her serious nature. The relationship between the estate owner and his poorer neighbors took a different form at Dornach from that at Wolfsberg. There a sort of armed truce prevailed, open, mutual hostility; deep-rooted dishonesty and guile on the part of the weak, obstinacy and relentless severity on the part of the strong.

"I only want my rights," the count would say and was merciless in the attainment of these rights.

"Rights?" said Hermann. "With what right does one demand an idea of rights from those who have always been forced to bow down to power?"

Maria agreed with him. She was, like him, a child of the new age; a sense of the intolerability of the suffering and the privation of others and the ardent desire to help had often seized her too. Now the power to satisfy it was in her hands. She felt a fervent gratitude to the one who had given it to her and who allowed her to exercise it under his guidance.

"Today is Tuesday, and the day of our family dinner," Hermann said one morning, as he entered the breakfast room. "Had you forgotten?"

She confessed, "Yes, completely forgotten. So a week has gone by since our arrival?"

"An entire week. It seems to me to have flown by like a blissful moment . . . . And to you, Maria? Not too slowly?"

"No, no," she said softly.

He put his arms around her. "If it continues like this, we will suddenly be a couple of old people. Unforeseen, age will someday surprise us, but I fear neither it nor death. It is good to die after a well-lived life in which one has never been mistaken in those one holds dearest and best, as I can never be mistaken in you."

"What do you mean by that? What is the substance of what you ask of me?" she asked.

Hermann gazed into her eyes with a long look that sought understanding. "You already know: for the time being — an exchange. For my boundless love, your boundless trust. '*Espérant mieux*' was, I believe, the motto of Antoine Latour."[8]

Maria bowed her head. "You are so good. You have the patience with me that I asked of you," she whispered, after a short silence, and suddenly hid her face in his shoulder.

"The horses! Your horses from Wolfsberg," Lisette's loud voice could now be heard in the next room, and she herself sidled in, smiling and caustic, submissive and resentful, as always in Hermann's presence. In her eyes he was nothing but a robber with special privileges who had stolen her "child." She had forgotten every melancholy hour she had spent in Maria's birthplace, and in Dornach now represented Wolfsberg as the promised land. She received every letter, every package that came from there as though it were a greeting from the abode of the blessed.

"And Georg brought them, your dear horses, old Georg, who can hardly wait to kiss your hand, Countess, my child," she added in a sentimental tone. The same horses that she had hated fiercely as a constant menace to Maria's life and her yet unbroken limbs, and the same Georg she had loathed, because he had saddled these horses, now stood high in her favor.

From the window she watched the "child," who, filled with happiness at the impending reunion with her four-legged darlings, was hurrying across the courtyard at Hermann's side. "Without a hat, without gloves, naturally," grumbled Lisette and gave in to her habit of talking to herself in an undertone as soon as she was alone. "Who looks after you here, little bird? Certainly not the infatuated count — he thinks of nothing, sees nothing, he's stupid and blind with love."

She entered the study, rang the bell, and ordered the housemaid to bring Maria the things she had forgotten. Then she took up the occupation that had been interrupted a while ago. This consisted of clearing out the contents of a rosewood rococo desk with bronze ornamentation and inlaid panels of old Saxon porcelain. Lisette removed the paper and cotton wrappings from countless invaluable items, some quite tiny, candy boxes, various receptacles, ivory carvings, seals, and small bottles, and placed everything on a table near the delicate little glass cupboard that hung on the wall and was destined to receive these small treasures. Almost all of these objects awakened in the old woman an unhappy memory of their previous owner, Maria's mother. They were all presents from the count. He had sent them home from Paris, where he had been briefly employed on a special diplomatic mission, as tokens of his loving thoughts of her each day. And how they had made her happy, made her blissful! With what eagerness had the young wife sought above all the hastily scrawled note that usually accompanied these packages. Usually — not always . . . and then, when what she had awaited with the greatest longing did not appear, then the beautiful object had no charm for her, and the countess bent sadly over her little child and said, "He hasn't written to us today, Maria . . . ."

"She loved him too much. Yes, indeed." Lisette reflected, and her lips twisted into a spiteful smile. "You won't follow her example, my little bird," she murmured. "You have a different nature. If, in your marriage, one of you loses his head for love, it'll be the other one, not you."

"What are you laughing about?" asked Maria as she entered.

"Oh . . . it's nothing . . . at the funny saint here. What sort of saint is that?" She handed the mistress a box that was decorated with a little enamel picture by Petitot,[9] which portrayed a young faun wreathed with vine leaves.

Maria looked at it attentively for the first time; she was no admirer of art in miniature and had never had any particular interest in these trinkets. Now, however, she looked carefully and marveled at the delicate work of the French master, and, as she turned the little box this way and that, the cover sprang open at the pressure of her finger. The inside revealed a key wrapped in a scrap of silk; the arabesque design of the filigreed handle seemed to Maria to bear a resemblance to the inlaid decoration of the box she had received from her father the evening before her wedding and whose key was missing. However, she had no time to ascertain whether the two belonged together, because the arrival of her guests, at one o'clock sharp, an hour before lunch, was imminent.

And they drove up, punctual to the minute, two big ones and four little ones. At the last minute Wilhelm had allowed himself to be softened by the sad faces with which the younger scamps had accompanied their parents' preparations for departure and had brought them. They were, after all, still so stupid and would not miss any lessons, or hardly any. Father and mother pleaded earnestly that no trouble at all be taken for them, that they simply be allowed to run around in the garden. They were old enough to guard against a fall into the water or from a tree. They had no right to expect any consideration at the meal; they had been fed well at home, and, moreover, each of them had a piece of bread in his pocket to tide him over comfortably until the return home.

They experienced no such inhospitable treatment, however; rather, they were allowed to bring their bread ration to the horses. Maria drove their mother and two of them at a time around the grounds in the pony carriage, while the other two ran after them, racing against the dogs. At the table they received chairs next to one another, sat bolt upright, and behaved themselves in an exemplary manner. Excellently directed by the terse commands of their father and the warning or affirmative glances of their mother, they displayed, despite all their training, an appetite worthy of little redskins.

Maria had prepared herself for the delights of today's family gathering with unconfessed dread, and now she fulfilled the duties of the lady of the house with pleasure and almost enjoyed herself. Not only with the children. The worthy man, who, as she knew, met the costs of maintaining his numerous offspring with difficulty and nevertheless looked forward to their possible increase with simple resignation, the woman with her work-worn hands and the character of her ancient, aristocratic lineage in her fine features, who wore her cap with the colored ribbons and her faded twilled silk dress with such courageous perseverance, inspired in their new relative the heartfelt esteem that with her was a reliable harbinger of future friendship.

They parted soon after the meal. Hermann and Wilhelm drove to a farm two hours away in order to look at construction that had been undertaken there. Countess Wilhelmine and her children rumbled home in their newly painted little green wagon, which was pulled by farm horses.

Maria was left alone and wanted to make use of her solitude to take a walk through the park in order to reach a lovely vantage point Hermann had told her about. She took both of his hunting dogs with her as companions, flaxen, short-haired, very intelligent animals, who, already on the day of Maria's arrival, had understood that in the absence of the master there was now a mistress. They followed at her heels, their noses down, with ears hanging, and when something stirred in the meadow, in the bushes, in the dark shadows of the trees, they started back, raised their noses in the air, and sniffed, every sinew tensed to spring. One cry, however — "Down! Lord, Fly, down!" — and they would sadly drop their heads again and move forward, obedient to the commands of humans, resisting the laws of their own nature.

It was a cool afternoon; Maria made good progress, animated by a pleasant feeling of freedom. At home she would have been prohibited from taking a long walk alone, and she perceived her newly acquired independence as a great delight. Everything contributed to increasing her desire to wander: the cloudless sky that stretched blue above her; the bracing air, scented with resin, that swept down from the fir trees; the springtime songs of the birds in the branches; the beauty of the place itself through which Maria walked. It seemed to her that she was in an enchanted garden, which was tended by benevolent spirits. They had strewn the paths with sand, mown the meadows, trimmed the hedges, built the little bridges over the stream. They had moored the boats, pennants flying, to the banks of the pond, scrubbed shiny the windowpanes of the fisherman's house so that they glittered like gold in the sunset, and, after completing their work, disappeared without a trace.

Everything, everything, is here for my sake, Maria said to herself, and at the same time it flashed through her: if Tessin were standing here now and could see me in this little earthly paradise . . . .

She had wanted to ban him from her thoughts, was not able to, and — had made her peace with him.

What had been his crime, after all? Had he tried to deceive her, had he ever spoken a word of love to her? And yet she had been envied for his attentions to her and had felt herself enviable and had not analyzed the nature of his power over her.

The vague, inexplicable fear that had sometimes overcome her in his presence, under the spell of his eyes, rippled through her; a presentiment of future sorrow gripped her heart.

She was not aware of the time that had passed since she had begun her walk and was astonished when she, emerging from a grove of firs, saw the sun about to set. With redoubled speed she hurried toward her destination, a stone pine, around whose colossal trunk a light, carved spiral staircase led up to a circular balcony, over which the mighty tree spread its green, sheltering branches.

The young woman ran up the steps in order to catch a last glimpse of the departing daytime star from the lofty watchtower. The dogs followed. Suddenly it seemed to her that the stairs shook . . . she stopped and waited, leaning on the railing — the shaking continued. She had not caused it. There must be someone pacing to and fro above her, slowly and heavily. For a moment she thought of fleeing; it was entirely too isolated here. Immediately, however, she laughed at the cowardly impulse that might have mastered her. Who could it be? A hunter, at worst a poacher. But even so, what did she have to fear?

The dogs growled. The footsteps stopped; hers had been heard.

A few seconds later she stepped onto the platform in the midst of the furious barking of Lord and Fly, who had bounded on ahead of her.

"Hey, the dogs! Call off the dogs!" an agitated voice shrieked at her. The man who had uttered this cry pressed his back against the trunk of the tree and struck a blow with his walking stick at his attackers but did not hit them.

Maria had recognized him at first sight, despite the change in him. He was not in rags, as he had been on that winter night, but was dressed elegantly in a lightweight summer suit, with well-groomed hair and beard; his appearance would have been that of a remarkably attractive man if it were not for the expression of depravity and illness in his pale, gaunt face.

Maria, too, had grown pale. "Come here!" she ordered the dogs, who reluctantly obeyed, and said in a harsh tone to the stranger, "Only members of the household are allowed in the park. What do you want here?"

He had regained the assurance of which his fear had robbed him. He lifted his hat mockingly and replied, "I want the same thing you want — to admire the view, which is really quite charming. Let us fulfill the purpose of our walk."

"What insolence!" murmured Maria, and, extending her right arm imperiously, she added loudly, "Leave!"

"Excuse me," he responded, "I am staying. I must speak to you and would have requested a meeting with you, had not coincidence — or was it perhaps a secret inner voice? — led you here, dear sister."

Maria uttered a muffled cry and shrank back. The way this man now bowed slightly — he did it a certain way, with a motion of the head that she knew well, that was so dear and congenial in another . . . .

"It offends you that I permit myself to call you by this name, but — it applies to you, and through no fault of mine . . . . Stay," he urged, as Maria, appalled and distressed, suddenly turned to go. "Someday we will have to talk — why not today rather than tomorrow? What I have to tell you is quickly said. Our father betrayed my mother — as he did yours, by the way," he burst out mockingly.

"That is a lie!" Maria said, but he continued, not allowing himself to be interrupted.

"I do not reproach him; I do not accuse him at all. Our father has spent a lot of money on me — what a waste! He wanted to have me educated, have principles instilled in me. All in vain, because — I have his blood in my veins. That his son turned out too much like him filled the excellent man with indignation. Finally he withdrew his support. Strange reasoning, isn't it?" He broke into a laugh that gradually became violent coughing. Dark red flecks appeared on the handkerchief he pressed to his lips. "There," he said, "I'm finished. I've known too much in life, too much pleasure and too much misery. Now I'm finished, finished, do you hear? The snow shoveling trick brought me the last handout

29

from the count, the very last. Don't let me die like an animal; give me a place to stay, sister."

She stared at him as though lost. "Lies, lies! I don't believe — I don't believe you . . . ."

"That would certainly be the most comfortable solution, but you can't see it through. Just ask the count, my brother-in-law; he knows about me, Wolfi Forster — just tell him my name. I want to speak to him, that is, to both of you, tomorrow morning at ten o'clock in the fisherman's cottage by the pond. Be sure to come; otherwise I could cause trouble for you. Right now this cursed devil of an illness is sending me home to the village inn, where I've taken lodgings for the time being." He buttoned his coat; feverish chills shook him. "Good-bye."

With that he extended his hand to Maria; she pulled hers back with disgust. "Oh, dear sister," he cried, "you are even prouder than our esteemed and noble father!"

VII.

Hermann had listened in silence to the story of Maria's adventure in the park and had presented himself the next morning at the fisherman's house for the meeting with Wolfi.

"A very sick man, perhaps a dying man," he said on his return. "Whoever he may be, we cannot, at least for the present, refuse him the shelter he requests."

"We cannot — you mean, we are not permitted to," said Maria. "So this man has a right — "

"As much a right," he interrupted her, "as our pity confers on him."

"He inspires none in me; he is too impudent," she answered.

She scarcely enquired about what was done for him, although Lisette displayed quite a remarkable interest in the vagrant guest. He had been allocated rooms in the house of a forester's widow that was located on the edge of the forest but was still near enough to the village to enable the doctor to visit him daily. Lisette honored the latter, a very good-natured and very inquisitive elderly man, with her confidence. They sat next to each other at the bedside of the sick man, who, in the first few days, started up out of unconsciousness only to lapse into feverish delirium in which he laughed and prattled and divulged all the secrets of his poor corrupt soul.

The doctor literally drank in his every word. "Miss Lisette," he said one day, "secret family circumstances are being revealed to us here."

She smiled. "I've already been initiated, Doctor, and I don't need to pride myself on it. Whoever knows this family knows this wild scion, who was born at Wolfsberg. It would have been difficult enough to deny, considering the resemblance and the impertinent uproar his mother created before the count's wedding — as though others couldn't have made the same claim . . . . Ah, there's nothing to be said about that — " she broke off suddenly.

"Say it nevertheless, Miss Lisette; don't be embarrassed, just say it!"

Lisette responded with a small, coquettish shrug of the shoulders. "You can imagine for yourself. A gentleman like our count, such a handsome man, can he help it if women run after him? It's their own business and their own fault. A gentleman like that isn't going to play the saint."[10]

Dr. Weise agreed. He would have liked to make a downright improper joke in order to make the dazzling impression of a Don Juan on the elderly spinster. Because he was by nature a chaste man, however, nothing risqué occurred to him.

Lisette freshened the damp compress on Wolfi's forehead. "Such a handsome fellow and already dying," she sighed. "Quite sad, but, after all, it's the best thing for him and also for the others."

The doctor eyed his patient critically; he was breathing quietly now and seemed to be sleeping peacefully. "Well built, strong; he may yet hold out awhile."

"How long, for instance?"

"Difficult to say — wouldn't want to embarrass myself in front of the lady" — he bowed gallantly — "I think, though, with excellent care — in this healthy air — maybe two years yet."

The sick man opened his eyes and glared at him. "Fool," he said, as loudly as he could, "don't you see that I'm awake?"

"I see that you've regained consciousness and I congratulate you," said the doctor, not in the least offended.

"Two years, how many days is that? . . . Calculate . . . ." Wolfi began to count slowly, his voice grew weaker and weaker, and he fell asleep again.

"Already come to his senses," Lisette whispered. "I wouldn't have believed it. That was a fine cure of yours; you'll save him in the end. But then the first thing will be" — these words were accompanied by a significant gesture — "for him to depart."

"It will hardly come to that, Miss Lisette," replied the doctor and bowed even more gallantly than he had before.

Lisette, however, cast a glance at the small mirror that hung over the wardrobe and said to herself, "I really don't know why I wear such old-fashioned caps."

At the same time, at the manor house, Maria had gone to her desk with the intention of answering Wolfsberg's last letter. A letter rich with earnest and singular thoughts, full of deep feeling and tenderness, which she read again and again with pride and innermost gratification. Never had her father spoken to her as lovingly as he now wrote; he no longer feared spoiling her.

Sitting down at the desk, Maria noticed that the ornamental box that had belonged to her mother had been placed next to her writing-case.

It was an old acquaintance — Maria had seen it often, always in the same spot in her father's room, and had often admired its delicate ornamentation. The handle of the little key in the enamel box had seemed to be decorated with similar embellishments and filigree. She retrieved it from the little box and tried it in the lock. It fit, but resisted her attempts to turn it. The task required much patience and dexterity; at last the cover sprang open and the contents were revealed. These consisted of a torn notebook, whose yellowed pages were completely covered with fine, delicate writing, and some old letters, tied together with a faded ribbon. Maria pulled one of them out. Her father had written it to her mother during their engagement; the letter expressed the most ardent passion with a breathtaking eloquence. How these protestations, these vows must have convinced their reader and made her blissful! How rich was a life adorned by the love of such a man! And although it had ended early, it had been filled with what is most precious, most rare — complete happiness.

Maria reached for one of the pages on which she recognized her mother's own handwriting. It hung loosely from a silk thread that bound it to the others and was, like all the rest, a fragment. The whole thing was the remnant of a notebook that appeared to have been at one time rather thick. Bent and crumpled, the cover was still there. Maria smoothed it as well as she could. Its title, written in careful calligraphy, was "In Heaven," followed by a date, "1850." But the beautiful letters had been crossed out, disfigured as though by a child's destructive impulse, and an unsteady hand had taken great pains to add a drawing of the devil. Below this picture was written, almost illegibly, "The King of Heaven" and the date, "1858."

Maria read here and there a sentence, a line; her face grew dark; transfixed, she looked down at the mutilated pages. There the mute, dead symbols came to life and spoke, bearing witness to a pain long buried. Conquered, forgotten, that pain rose from its grave and moaned again its heart-rending laments and accusations.

They found an anguished echo in Maria's soul.

Once again, something had been destroyed for her: a belief that had made her happy . . . . Belief? No, a belief that is based on an error is a delusion. Maria was very inclined to mourn the loss of hers; the artistic element of her nature resisted the destruction of the ideal her father had once represented for her. Then she noticed a word written in the margin of one of the most ill-treated pages of the strange diary: *TRUTH*, in capital letters, enclosed in a graceful arabesque.

Maria did not look up again until she had absorbed the meaning of the last line that was even halfway comprehensible to her. Then she kissed the pages tenderly and repeatedly, carried them to the fireplace, burned them, and waited on her knees for the flames to die. The dead woman's secret was preserved in the heart of her child.

Some of the passages, taken out of context, that had imprinted themselves almost in their entirety on Maria's memory were as follows:

"I demand the truth from you. You must not lie. You cannot be faithful, cannot hold fast to what your heart has once captured. You are weak and help-less against your passions. At least be honest. Pity for the weak; contempt for the liar."

*

"Jealous is not the right word. If I were, would I love your Wolfi? Would I honor the memory of his mother? And I would have good reason to be jealous of her, because she loved you more than I do; I would not have sacrificed for you what she did: her parents, her home, honor and duty."

*

"When my daughter is grown, I will say to her: do not marry for love. We think that to be united with the one we love is heaven on earth. It is not true. What makes heaven a heaven? That a God reigns in it and — "

*

"If God were only as good to us as we are to our worthy servants, then He would have answered my prayers. Have I not faithfully fulfilled all my duties? Was I not devout and pious? If God were good and just, He would have an-swered my prayers. But there is no God at all in heaven, only a devil, and he is punishing me."

*

"Beloved, when our youth is past, when you have come back to me, and I have forgiven you everything, then we will read together what I now write, and take each other by the hand and laugh — and cry a little too."

*

". . . that you lead Alma astray — she has a conscience. It is only sleeping now, you have lulled it to sleep, you know how to do that . . . but it will awaken and then — "

*

"I don't believe it, I want to know, to convince myself, to lie in wait for you. I am a hunter now; you are both my timid prey . . . ."

"Sometimes I fear and sometimes I hope that I will lose my mind. We will not read my diary together, dearest beloved. I think that I must tear it up. The beautiful description of the blissful days — already gone. Torn into tiny, tiny pieces and let fly from the 'high balcony of the tower' . . . . How they scattered in the wind . . . . What did I think about? What? About my happiness or what? I don't know anymore . . . ."

*

The next time Hermann paid a visit to the forester's house, Maria accompanied him. The sick man recovered very slowly from the last severe attack of his illness. He lay, completely exhausted, half waking, half sleeping, took only with reluctance the nourishment he was given, and counted incessantly on his fingers how many months, weeks, days he had yet to live. The calculation was too difficult for him, however, and would not come out right. Toward all who approached him, including Hermann, he exhibited hostile suspicion and a sullen and gruff demeanor that very often exhausted even the patience of his long-suffering doctor.

Only when Maria appeared at his bedside, did his forehead smooth, and he smiled; beneath his small, black moustache, his teeth gleamed, as young and healthy as those of a child. In the depths of his dark eyes an uncanny glow was kindled. "Dear — " he would say and then make a long pause. "Are you afraid, are you afraid of the word I could say now?" asked his spiteful and threatening look. But hers held him spellbound. Proudly and coldly it rested upon him, and he would murmur, confused, "Dear Countess."

She came regularly, but not on particular days, twice a week, as she returned from her errands in the village. There she had visited the poor and the sick, had usually also gone to the school and listened to an hour of lessons. She had criticized, praised, given generously, and with all that had only continued what her mother-in-law had introduced — although not exactly in the same spirit.

Countess Agathe had demanded something in return from those on whom she had conferred her aid: "You will receive this only on condition that you stay away from the tavern hereafter." "You will receive that only on condition that you fulfill your religious obligations punctually from now on."

Maria, on the other hand, not only set no conditions, she even refused thanks; its usually effusive expression was distasteful to her. With that she annoyed the clergymen and the teachers, who were accustomed to reaping indirectly their share of the countess's benevolence, and devalued her gifts in the eyes of the recipients. How highly should something be esteemed when it was to be had for nothing?

"To give with one hand and to stretch out the other to take," said Maria to Hermann, "disgusts me."

"I don't understand that," he replied. "What these people lack above all else, what they should be taught above all else, is a sense of duty. You will not awaken that with charity."

"Will I awaken it when I suggest a transaction to them, an exchange?"

"It is much more likely. When you do good for someone and as compensation for that ask that he do good, you can arouse the concept of equity in him, a notion of what duty is. And when you have done that, you have been far more useful to him than when you have eased his misery for the moment."

She had to admit that and did it gladly. She was happy to be convinced by him, to bow to his greater experience, to acknowledge his straightforward worldly wisdom. A beautiful life could be led at his side, an active and useful life. There was time in it for everything, including the cultivation of her beloved art.

Late in the summer Count Wolfsberg was to arrive for a long visit with his children. Shortly before the day on which they expected him, however, he canceled his visit. He was obliged to represent a man of high rank at a foreign court temporarily and would have to postpone his visit to Dornach for three months.

The equanimity with which Maria received this news astonished Hermann, as did the silence she had maintained since her marriage on the subject of Alma Tessin. He himself had brought her a letter from the woman who had once been her best friend; it had remained unanswered. Hermann did not ask. Chance, he thought, which the blind call blind, has surely been at work here and has informed Maria of things that had previously been carefully hidden from her. How it had happened was still a mystery to him; he expected the future to provide an explanation.

The fall came; the Christmas holidays drew near. Snow and ice covered the meadows and the ponds; nature was dead — seemingly dead. But beneath Maria's heart, a new life stirred and struggled vigorously and forcefully toward the daylight.

VIII.

An anxious day at Dornach.

The portly woman who had been staying at the manor for a week, whose meals were served in her room, and who, to the annoyance of the butler, polished off a bottle of Bordeaux at lunch and at supper each day, had been at the bedside of the countess since two o'clock in the morning. At the train station a carriage awaited the arrival of the express train that was to bring the distinguished doctor from Vienna. Dr. Weise had set himself up in Lisette's maidenly chamber and, whenever a noise was heard in the hall, would step out and say to whomever was passing by, "I'm here — just so you know — in case a doctor should be necessary, you know where to find him."

No one took any notice of him; he was completely uninteresting. Eager attention was directed exclusively at the women who had been given the opportunity to be of assistance in the vicinity of the delivery room.

In the afternoon, as he stood at the foot of his wife's bed of pain, his face agitated, Hermann was forced to leave by Cousin Wilhelmine.

Now they were in his study, his cousin and he. Wilhelm had taken a seat in the middle of the sofa, had bent forward, and was occupying himself with cracking his thick, red fingers. Hermann paced restlessly up and down in front of the bookcase that took up the whole length of one wall and either whistled appallingly out of tune or sank into a gloomy silence or stood still in front of Wilhelm and stared at him.

Twilight had fallen; the valet appeared.

"What do you want?" asked his master.

"To light the lamp."

"We don't need a lamp," Hermann uttered with difficulty, and Wilhelm thought, "The poor fellow is close to tears."

"Today," he said, after a pause, "we caught three martens in the trap," to which his cousin responded, "What time is it?"

"It has just struck five."

"Good heavens! Then the doctor from Vienna should already be here." He rang, and it was an incredibly long time until a footman finally entered and announced that the doctor had arrived and that Lisette had taken him to the countess.

An hour passed, during which the time rolled on in leaden waves and Wilhelm gave up his futile attempts to distract Hermann's thoughts. Suddenly the latter stood still and listened. He had recognized the hurried footsteps that were approaching; they were Wilhelmine's. She threw open the door. The adjacent room was brightly lit, and at the threshold her figure stood out as if against a radiant golden background.

"Hermann?" she called questioningly into the darkness. "Come, Hermann, come — you have a son!"

"And Maria — "

"Doing well, thank God."

He rushed toward her and lifted up the stout woman in his arms and shouted with joy.

"What are you doing?" she said. "Get hold of yourself. She is still weak. If you do not get hold of yourself, you cannot see her."

"Oh — I'll — " He made an enormous effort at self-control, drew himself up, embraced his cousin, and pulled her with him as he went. "Wilhelm, send a telegram to my mother and to my father-in-law," he called back, still breathless. He covered the entire distance on tiptoe, entered Maria's darkened room as inaudibly as a sylph, and would have preferred to assume the form of a cloud to approach her.

She lay very still, was pale — even her lips were pale — and looked infinitely tired. But she smiled at him, happily, tenderly, and gently. His heart almost overflowed with emotion — but she hated to be pitied. He could not say anything; he only kissed her hands softly and, as he did so, glanced with a certain embarrassment at a white bundle of fabric, lace, embroidery, and ribbons that was placed beside her.

"I congratulate you on a splendid boy," the distinguished doctor said to him as he entered.

"Where?" stammered Hermann, and Wilhelmine burst out, "Good Lord, there, of course!"

There — to be sure. From beneath the embroidery and the lace, something peeped out. A small brownish-red face with a wrinkled forehead, light-sensitive, tightly shut little eyes, a nose covered with countless small, yellow dots, and a tiny mouth. Little fists were visible, too, which had disproportionately long fingers and the most delicate and slender nails. So that was the "splendid boy," that was the "son."

Hermann was astonished and kissed his hands too.

Maria recovered slowly, and Dr. Weise, who, after the departure of the doctor from Vienna, had been put in charge, never tired of prescribing as much rest as possible. "Especially for her nerves. No excitement, Count, Miss Lisette, Miss Klara, no excitement!" He was pleased that the christening could not take place for the next fourteen days, because Count Wolfsberg, who insisted on acting as godfather to his grandson in person, was unable to arrive any earlier.

The count wrote or sent a telegram daily, and it seemed to Hermann that these messages from her father caused Maria discomfort. Eventually he no longer ventured to communicate them to her. Now, however, she asked every evening, "Is Father coming?" and when the answer was finally "Yes," her cheeks flamed a feverish red. She closed her eyes; her heart beat quickly and shallowly; an inexpressible anxiety came over her.

"What is it?" Hermann asked. "Maria, what is troubling you? There is something that is troubling you and that you are keeping from me."

She sighed deeply. "Let it be," she said. "We will never speak of it. Go now; it's late. I must rest and gather strength for tomorrow."

"Certainly," he said and was already on tiptoe and assuming the sylph-like gait he used these days.

Maria motioned him back. "There is one thing I'd like to ask of you — tell it to Father. The child shall be called Hermann, Hermann Wolfgang . . . . Do you understand me? And may he be like you, dear."

He left happy; he made himself the guardian of the peace and quiet she had asked for. Nevertheless, he was not able to produce more than silence on all sides. A silence so deep that Maria could hear the breathing of the baby, whose cradle stood close to her bed. He was unbelievably well-behaved, cried only as much as was proper for a two-week-old youngster, took his nourishment from his mother's breast, slept, and smiled often in his sleep.

And the sight of his tranquillity was the only real comfort Maria's soul could find in this last night before the reunion with her father. A reunion and yet not a reunion — after all, it was another man who would appear before her, not the one she had loved and adored, but one who had lied, betrayed, and killed — one she had condemned.

The next morning he was there, not in the least fatigued, despite the long journey. He had relinquished the carriage waiting for him at the station to his valet and had come on foot. A brisk walk in the dewy morning was what he needed after two nights spent in the railway car.

His son-in-law ran to meet him; the two men shook hands. Wolfsberg asked first about Maria and then immediately about water to wash himself and allowed himself to be taken to the rooms prepared for him.

Half an hour later he stood before his daughter, dressed with inimitably elaborate carelessness, fragrant with cleanliness and *eau de toilette*, an expression of joyful emotion on his resolute face. He patted Maria on the cheek and said, half to Hermann, half to her, "She's grown thin."

She would have liked to cry out, "I know what you did and I will never forgive you!" — but the sight of him, his voice, his fleeting kiss on her forehead exercised their old power. She succumbed to it almost without resistance. "He is, after all, my father," she thought.

The count gave his grandson the appropriate attention, seated himself at Maria's bedside, and began to talk to her, more about himself than about her, frankly, confidingly, quite as though he were speaking to an equal whose company he had long and painfully done without. He had noticed her coldness and uneasiness immediately. He attributed it at once to the correct cause: Maria had learned something that diminished him in her eyes. From whom? Wolfsberg was too good a judge of human nature to entertain even the shadow of a suspicion about Hermann. "What difference does it make," he thought, "by whom your illusions about me were destroyed, you poor child; they are gone. You must learn to take me as I am and to realize that you can still be proud of me, nevertheless." Then he deployed all of his purposeful charm, put himself in the best light — in that he confessed to a mistake, to committing some act of injustice. With the air of an inferior, he lowered himself to her whom he had comprehended with just a glance. The regaining of shaken influence, the resecuring of wavering affection was at stake — in a word: a conquest.

How well he succeeded in his task! How his daughter, when he left Castle Dornach after a short stay, loved him more than ever! The strong man was helpless against his passions — was that not a reason to pity him? And who had seen his struggles? Gifted with so fine a sense of all that was noble, what must he suffer from the awareness of his fallibility! He was not one of those who are cowardly enough to deceive themselves about their shortcomings. This awareness of his own limitations, she told herself, was probably the source of his harsh rejection of Tessin. Perhaps he saw — at least in one sense — a resemblance between himself and Tessin. He wanted to protect his daughter from the painful disillusionment he had caused her mother.

Maria still cherished the memory of the departed one well and faithfully, although in her eyes her mother was no longer the victim of a crime, but the martyr to an unavoidable fate, a saint transfigured by suffering, in front of whose portrait she would lapse into contemplative devotion.

Gradually her cheerfulness returned and grew with the feeling of increasing strength and recovered health. She had insisting on nursing her child herself, although "no one" did so nowadays and although the doctors advised her against it. But she knew perfectly well what she was able to take on.

Her cousin Wilhelm displayed an admiration for her that manifested itself in the most exceptional attentions. The entire winter he came every evening on horseback, whatever the weather, halted in the castle courtyard, asked, "How is everything?" and, after receiving an answer, returned home on his plump brown mare. As soon as the roads were passable again, the Tuesday family dinners began anew.

After the first one, Wilhelm had pulled his cousin into a window recess and whispered mysteriously to him, "Your wife was always splendid — but only now has she become genial. That's because of the child, yes, my friend. One speaks of the heart's chamber — that's completely wrong: it has many chambers. Here and there there is one that has been open since childhood. The others open little by little — I'm speaking only of good people, of course — and a child sometimes brings the key to the most important one in its little hand."

Maria did in fact seem to have found a serene happiness in her marriage. And was she not to be envied above a thousand others? Worshipped and adored by a man whom she sincerely esteemed, mother of a rosy child, beautiful without being vain and highly talented without being ambitious, endowed abundantly enough with earthly possessions to be able to satisfy the liveliest beneficent impulses, she was one of fortune's chosen ones. She herself considered it her duty to count herself among them.

Earlier than Hermann had wanted to permit it, Maria had appeared again in the cottages of the poor; however, he had to exhort and to urge her again and again before she made the decision to cross Wolfi's threshold once more after a long absence.

Although he had barely recovered from a renewed, violent attack of his illness, he nevertheless got up to receive her and came several steps to meet her. A feeble expression formed around his mouth as he smiled at her. "Finally, Countess," he said in a weak, hoarse voice, "finally! As you can see, I'm doing better. Your great doctor gives me only about five hundred days to live, but I intend to be a burden to you longer than the learned man imagines; I — "

Hermann interrupted him with the request that he make the confession that had been on his mind.

"But don't spoil my pleasure, Countess," said Wolfi.

"What pleasure?"

"That of listening when you play the piano . . . . You're amazed! That miserable fellow, Wolfi, has an ear for music — particularly for the music you play." He struck his breast with the palm of his hand. "A soothing remedy, Countess. I've dragged myself by all sorts of roundabout ways to the neighborhood of the castle, to the summerhouse behind the lilac bushes, and listened. Yes, that was music! A cold shiver runs down one's back at the sound of it, and that's the way it should be. I had never believed you capable of so much passion — you have it here," he put his hand to his heart, "and in your fingers, and I would have had it too, would certainly have become an artist . . . . But would it have been possible? What, an artist — a rogue! One of the great count's precepts: Nothing comes of the artist except when the rogue in him provides the motivation for it. Well, then — I request free admission to the summerhouse and also that the dogs and the servants receive orders not to disturb me there when I come, which will not happen too often. But may I? May I?" he repeated impatiently.

Maria hesitated. "A concealed audience is not very pleasant."

"Excuses! What do you care about an audience when you're playing?"

Hermann put in a word in Wolfi's favor, and his wish was granted.

From this day on Maria prolonged her visits to the sick man. "A person who has preserved his receptivity to the beautiful can't be entirely bad," she thought and viewed it as her mission to save the soul that would be summoned so soon before his eternal judge. She considered the cynicism with which he received her admonitions to be a loathsome mask and the objections he raised to be pitiful boasting.

One afternoon she found him in great excitement. He was occupied with reading a letter and received her with the words, "Don't I have distinguished correspondents, eh? Just look at the signature."

She read with pained astonishment, "Felix Tessin."

Wolfi put the letter in his pocket. "Yes," he said carelessly, "that one answers a fellow, remembers the youthful friendship of long ago. An incredulous smile? You can't forget the streetsweeper; he made an indelible impression on you. But that episode of my eventful life was preceded by others. Hey, hey — what's the matter?" He stopped.

Maria had a way of raising her head and looking silently at those who did or said something that displeased her that threw even the most impudent into confusion.

Wolfi experienced it now. "Have no fear! Why the display of dignity?" he sneered. "I have no intention of entering into details; I am only saying that we were friends. Felix and I studied in Heidelberg together — don't ask me what — and were expelled together. Tessin did not trouble himself with the number of ancestors a fellow had, but with the number of women's hearts he conquered and with the sword he wielded. He learned to appreciate mine during a surprise attack on him staged by an offended husband . . . . Yes, we were friends!"

"And each worthy of the other," said Maria and turned to hide her flushed cheeks. How could she have spoken these words? Had she not long since overcome her bitterness toward Tessin?

She stood up and left the room.

Lisette, who had accompanied her this time, heaped reproaches on Wolfi.

He, however, watched the tall figure from the window as it slowly disappeared behind the trees of the park, and he muttered through his teeth, "Oh, your majesty, I would give my last spark of life for one spot upon your ermine!"

IX.

One more autumn in the country, one more Christmas holiday at Dornach, which Countess Agathe spent with her children, reveling in the sight of her grandson. After the advent of the new year, they dispersed. Hermann and Maria traveled to Vienna to spend the winter, and Countess Agathe returned to her wilderness, but not without reminding the young people that one also has responsibilities to society. During the long years of the countess's widowhood there had been no festivities in the old Dornach palace, which an ancestor with a love of splendor had built for the hospitality of his descendants. Every evening the heavy gate had opened only for the respectable carriage of a matron or the venerable coach of the canonesses and had closed again behind it at ten o'clock, accompanied by the deep bows of the yawning doorkeeper, who had little by little come to the conclusion that the purpose of life is to rest.

All that was now to change, far more radically than the master and mistress of the house had intended. Their resolution to resist the pressure to participate in everything now proved itself impracticable; soon they were caught up in the social whirl. The world said to them, as to all its children, "Give yourself to me entirely; half-measures are of no use to me." And — Maria, at least, complied with the world's wishes, and in return she enjoyed intoxicating triumphs very different from those she had experienced as a young girl.

When she had earlier added up the sum of all that was asked of her, the answer was "to please." Now, on the other hand, everyone seemed to have just one wish, one ambition: to please *her*. One smile, one amiable word was a blessing; the slightest preference shown to one made a hundred others envious.

The first Dornach ball had earned unanimous praise. A second had aroused rapture. Now a third was to take place two days before Lent.

Someone who had until now carefully avoided Maria's presence endeavored to obtain an invitation to this ball: Felix Tessin. She had at first been grateful to him for his reserve, but finally she told herself that there was something more conspicuous about it than all the trite attentions paid to her by young and old.

What right did he have to make an exception of himself? Had the slightest thing ever happened between them that allowed him to behave otherwise toward her than everyone else did?

It almost pleased her when she received his visiting card one day and could send him an invitation to the ball. It was time that he gave up his unusual position. Just recently Hermann had said, "Tessin has not yet gotten over his defeat; he is sulking" — and as Maria had looked at him, astonished and dismayed, he had added calmly, "I would have relinquished you for any good man you had preferred to me, but not for Tessin. I would rather have shot him than allowed him to make you his bride."

Maria forced herself to assume an air of indifference. "What — you have discovered something about Count Tessin's failed attempt to assure himself in the simplest manner of my father's support? I congratulate you! No one except you noticed that little diplomatic blunder."

"So even I was once sharp-sighted," was Hermann's answer. "Love works wonders."

Maria remembered this conversation often as the hour approached when she would receive Tessin as a guest in her house. And what resolutions she made! With what ease did she wish to meet him and to strike immediately the cool and amiable tone that would prevail between them from now on.

The Monday before Lent arrived. It was nine o'clock; Maria had finished dressing and had gone into the nursery to say good night to the little one. He awakened as she bent over him, laughed happily, and reached with both hands for the glittering tiara on her head. She evaded him, kissed him, put him back to sleep, and whispered to him, "You are my dearest and best, after all."

Then she made her way to the party rooms, lit bright as day and fragrant with flowers. All was still silent and empty. Only in the conservatory, where dinner would be served, the head gardener from Dornach and his assistants were occupied with arranging a group of palms. And in the gallery, the head steward, with the ceremonious solemnity of one presiding over a cabinet meeting, issued his orders to the valets in their black dress coats and the footmen in gold braid and powdered wigs.

In the cool ballroom Hermann paced up and down in animated conversation with the conductor of the orchestra, a famous and amiable artist. As Maria approached, both stood still, and the musician cried out involuntarily, "How beautiful you look, Countess!"

"Don't I?" she responded, accepting his admiration with the same frankness with which he had expressed it. "This lace — a symphony of stitches; the tiara, one of Köchert's[11] masterpieces, magnificent, yet light, I hardly feel it — all gifts from my husband." And the least of them, she thought. What are gifts to him, after all? He was hers entirely, his first and last thoughts belonged to her, and what ornamented and made her life rich, from the greatest to the smallest, was the work of this man, who, though in possession of her, still strove longingly for her love.

Overcome with boundless gratitude, she was glad to be so beautiful, glad that today many would think him fortunate. With shining eyes, she looked in the mirror . . . . She could be satisfied with herself. Never had a dress been more becoming to her than this colorful-colorless one, a mixture of gray and violet for which there is no name. The costly, gold-embroidered lace fabric she had just praised encircled the neck of the bodice, formed a narrow band between the shoulder and the upper arm, and flowed, skillfully gathered, down from the waistband to the long train lined with heavy gold brocade. The noble form, re-splendent in its delicate abundance, seemed surrounded by a shimmering golden cloud, and the calm and stately grace of her movements was a joy to the eye.

Gradually the salons filled. High-spirited or weary, with a merry, expectant air or with an expression of boredom, the arriving guests surged in. The few hundred people who constitute genuine high society met once again at one and the same place — the flower of the nobility, the heads and relations of ancient families that had kept their blood pure of any intermixture with those of lesser birth.

There they stand, forming a large group, the famous Viennese *comtesses*, unique in their manner. The conversation of some is so unconstrained and so un-refined that it is not easy to recognize their naiveté. It is nothing but slang; they come by it easily. The one learns it from her father, the other from her brother, and the third from her friends. In reality, however, they have been carefully tended since their first breath, sheltered from the sight of anything ugly or evil, have grown up ignorant of misery and guilt. And now they are being intro-duced to the life for which everything that had preceded it was only the prepa-ration; they are approaching its threshold as though it were that of the gates of heaven and they knock bravely.

And the young men — all educated, although not always much more so than is necessary to pass the officers' examination. Many a one has shared a schoolbench with the son of his father's tailor or distiller and owes many a hard-won good grade to the desire not to be repeatedly outdone by a plebeian. But whether they plan to forget what they have learned as soon as possible and to live only for pleasure, or whether they perceive themselves to be budding field marshals, ambassadors, or cabinet members, the conviction that the world could only wish them well animates them all, and they enter like young kings entering their realms.

"Watch how they bow," Hermann said to his father-in-law. "A flourishing throng of newly commissioned lieutenants and attachés has just pushed itself through the crowd in order to pay its respects to the lady of the house. They stand motionless — only their arms are somewhat more rounded and their shoulders raised a bit more than usual. A slight jerk, the head inclines (by no means too low!) for a quarter of a second — respects have been paid."

43

"Fashionable," said Wolfsberg. "The fellows have all been dipped according to the same recipe and frozen stiff with elegance."

"And there is so much good hidden beneath the antics, so much honesty, ability, courage, and — how often — talent!"

"If they only knew what to do with it — good evening, Princess," he interrupted himself, returning with a deep bow the amiable nod of a stately, well-preserved lady.

"I'm looking for a seat on the platform between a couple of neighbors who are not too awfully obsessed by maternal ball mania. A seat for a fly on the wall, my dear Count," she said, laughing and in an excellent mood, although she knew that at the first sound of the violins she would be seized by an almost irresistible desire to whirl one more time — one last time — in the round dance. Oh, if only she were not ashamed to do it in front of her seventeen-year-old daughter . . . .

The arrival of the court was announced; Hermann hurried to meet the exalted guests on the steps, and shortly thereafter Maria opened the ball on the arm of a young archduke.

During the first dances, encircled and crowded by her guests, busy with her duties as the lady of the house, she had not yet seen the man she had been thinking of incessantly since the party had begun. Suddenly she thought she sensed his presence. He is here, she said to herself, and saw him. A dreadful confusion overcame her. His demonic good looks struck her as though for the first time.

He stood next to Countess Dolph's armchair, in animated conversation with her. The animation was hers. She was lively and stimulated; a red tinge flushed her withered cheeks; a merry, satirical smile played around her lips; her sharp features were lit up with an expression of the satisfaction she felt only in conversation with truly intelligent men. Tessin spoke little, but each of the short sentences he uttered seemed to arouse a world of ideas in the appreciative mind of the countess.

He broke off the conversation when his searching glance met Maria's, and came to her. They exchanged a few civilities, and he asked her for the next polka.

"I will give you the third — with my cousin, Countess Wolfsberg; I have just been told that she has no partner."

Tessin bowed and went to engage the young countess, one of the least gifted of her sex, for whom every ball was an exercise in sitting.

The cotillion, in which Tessin participated, offered him at last the opportunity for compensation that he had desired; he happily availed himself of it. Apparently by chance, a figure in the dance in which one must choose a partner brought him together with Maria. With passionate haste he took her in his arms. "Again, at last!" he said so loudly that Maria was alarmed, and then they were whirling, and her breath mingled with his, and his mouth brushed against her hair, and he pressed her to him and said, "I have avoided you, Countess, out of concern for my peace of mind," and she responded with a voice that seemed strange even to her and was harsh and uncertain . . . no, no, she had not wanted to receive him this way . . . . "And what safeguards it now?"

"Nothing, but I will attempt to gain it — that is, fortify it — far from you."

She laughed, "At what end of the earth?"

Instead of answering, he whispered to her, quickly, rashly, "It would have been good to have kept silent now too, as I was silent when others slandered me to you — don't deny it," he forestalled the objection she wanted to raise, " — slandered, and when you became the wife of another. It would have been heroic, I know, to go silently into exile — but I am not able to bring myself to such lofty virtue, and you should know — "

"So, you are really going into exile," she interrupted him. "Then I feel very sorry for little Nicolette."

She should not have said that! Oh, how clearly she saw that once it was too late, once it had been said, and mocking triumph flashed from the eyes of this experienced reader of hearts, who, in an entirely different and careless tone, asked, "Ah, the little one — you remember her? Wasn't she sweet?"

She did not speak to him again that evening, which he, which she herself had spoiled, whose memory was painful to her. She heard that he had accepted an "exotic" post and would leave Austria and Europe for years, probably very soon, perhaps already in a few weeks; the date had not yet been set.

Almost every day the restless conviviality in which they lived brought them together. They encountered each other on the ice, in the Prater, at dinners, at parties. And he, with consummate skill, with unwavering self-control, always contrived to be where she was and then to occupy himself with everyone except her. He zealously paid court to this or that flirtatious woman in Maria's presence; he squandered the treasures of his intellect and his wit on pretty *comtesses* who were a dime a dozen.

This was so strange, so unexpected after his bold attempt at making a declaration at the ball. She made light of it, found it childish, unworthy of her and of him, and nevertheless took up the challenge he offered her. To be sure, she was more occupied with him than was proper, thought about him — constantly! At first she struggled against this foolish obsession, but then she remembered the wise words, "We free ourselves from our passions when we think them." *From our passions* — how much easier, then, from a whim. Moreover, Tessin was soon to depart, and how quickly the little war they had waged with one another, as well as the caprice that had caused it, would then be forgotten.

Countess Dolph, one of whose senile vanities, as she herself put it, was to be compared with the Marquise du Deffand, called Tessin, who appeared regularly in her well-upholstered salon, which was carefully secured against the tiniest of drafts, her Horace Walpole.[12] She sang his praises in every key, and a huge chorus of lovely ladies joined in. Tessin had never been so exclusively and triumphantly in fashion as he was now that his prestige was heightened by the fact that he was about to depart.

Those who were ignorant on principle, who were the sworn enemies of geography, began to cultivate this despised science. Maps of Asia were studied intently in aristocratic houses, and the routes that Tessin should or could take were marked on them with colored pencils. An unprecedented desire for travel stirred suddenly in a hundred young female hearts.

It goes without saying that the evenings at Countess Dolph's, which otherwise possessed little attraction, were visited until the end of Lent like a sacred shrine. In the large apartment that the countess had kept in her brother's house, the hospitably opened row of rooms stood almost empty; however, the small chamber where the lady of the house received her favorite was always overflowing.

The count avoided these gatherings because Tessin was their focus, and Maria appeared as rarely as she could without making her absence conspicuous. Once, however, she arrived after the opera, accompanied by Hermann, and Wolfsberg appeared shortly after they did. He was in an ill mood; around his mouth lay the malevolent expression that Maria had once feared and that was even now unpleasant to her, since it betrayed a harshness toward lesser beings to which someone in a position of superiority, such as he, should not give way. He strode through the crowd into the vicinity of Countess Dolph, who was reclining in her well-cushioned armchair at the end of the room and jesting with Tessin, who sat on a stool next to her. A small court of particularly ardent followers surrounded them and participated occasionally in their conversation.

"Begum Somru and Dyce," said Wolfsberg to his daughter as he passed, and she responded, "No, Stuwer's successors — they're setting off conversational fireworks."[13]

The count shook his sister's hand, honored several of the ladies with his obliging attention, and noticed only after a while that Tessin had risen and was awaiting the count's response to his greeting.

Now he looked at him. Their glances crossed like unsheathed swords. The younger one did not lower his eyes, and Wolfsberg said, "Are you ready to depart?"

"I've been ready for four weeks now, your Excellency."

"So much the better, since you will certainly not be here that much longer. What do you think?"

"Always what your Excellency thinks."

"In every respect," interjected the little Countess Felicitas Soltan, who was called Fée and who was one of Wolfsberg's decided favorites. He enjoyed listening to the fountain of nonsense that bubbled from her pretty mouth and declared it to be a most agreeable noise, which relaxed him. Wealthy and orphaned, Fée had been married at sixteen by her relatives to a much older man, who made her a widow two years later. Now she enjoyed her young life and the

46

privilege she had bestowed upon herself of saying whatever crossed her mind. It had caused quite a sensation before Lent that she had turned down seven proposals of marriage because, according to her own admission, she had been "head over heels" in love with Tessin since childhood. Recently he had paid conspicuous attention to her for several days and now neglected her again just as conspicuously.

Maria saw through his game. She knew perfectly well whose consternation it was designed to arouse and that it had been dropped without further ceremony when it had failed to achieve its secret purpose.

Little Fée called to her and compelled her to sit next to her. "Did you hear," she asked, "how soon Tessin will abandon us? You may all be sorry about it if you like. I won't be sorry — I'm going to follow him."

Everyone laughed, and Tessin said, shrugging his shoulders, "You would have great difficulty, Countess. You don't have any idea which route you would have to take."

Fée's delicate child's face assumed a serious expression. "I'll simply ask; I'll drive to the train stations; I'll write to every stationmaster in the four corners of the earth."

"Even worse," Tessin replied, and his eyes rested upon her with merciless scorn, "for only in the fifth will you find scholars who can read your handwriting."

She searched for an answer and found none. "See how he is with me," she whispered to her neighbor. Her mouth quivered; she jumped up and said, with a sob in her voice, "The heat's unbearable here!"

Maria followed her. They both went to the window; Fée pressed her burning forehead against the glass. Tears streamed down her cheeks.

Half an hour later the Dornachs left the gathering and were passed on the steps by Tessin.

"I do not understand," Hermann said to him, "how you can find pleasure in making a woman who loves you look ridiculous."

"Who loves me?" Tessin responded, with an irritation that was unjustified by either the words or the tone in which they were spoken. "The love of a little weathervane."

"The deuce! Surely *you* don't reproach anyone for inconstancy?"

"I certainly do," Tessin said emphatically.

The following morning Hermann received a telegram from his mother's spiritual advisor, Father Schirmer. He had taken it upon himself to inform him that the countess was ill — although not seriously so.

The decision to depart that same evening was made immediately. The necessary arrangements were made; the child and his nurse were sent back to Dornach under Lisette's care.

Maria accompanied the little one to the train station, took leave of Aunt Dolph, and sent word to her father in his office. Upon returning home, she entered the nursery and left it again quickly — it made a painful impression on her. She went to Hermann's room; he had gone to see the man who managed his business affairs and had left a message not to expect him before dinner at seven o'clock.

Now Maria leaned back, a little tired, in the armchair at her desk. Throughout the entire recent past she had clung to her love for her child, had spent every free hour that her strenuous worldly life allowed her with Hermann. Soon she would live only for both of them, distracted by nothing, with no demands on her time other than those of the justified, holy affection that had entered her life as though to take the place of that, now completely changed, for two others: her father and the only female friend she had thought she possessed.

"I am rich enough," she said to herself and had the feeling that a few more hours would have to pass until she would be able to appreciate these riches fully. Then the inexplicable longing that now gripped her soul again and again would have disappeared, and she would be free . . . free . . . .

The door of the parlor adjacent to her study was opened; footsteps hurried through it; a valet entered, as well as, at almost the same time, the man he announced: Count Tessin.

X.

"Excuse me, Countess," he said, pausing where he stood in the doorway, "for not allowing you sufficient time to have me sent away. But I heard that you are leaving today, and I urgently need to speak to you."

It was impossible in the presence of the servant to refuse him admittance. Maria went to meet the visitor in the parlor and sat down at the little table where her needlework lay. She summoned all her strength in order to maintain a calm demeanor and offered Tessin a chair opposite her sofa.

Good heavens! How disconcerted she felt, how strange! Her tongue was paralyzed, an iron fist choked her, her heart pounded, her pulse raced — and this mad rebellion of her entire being was caused — oh, shame and transgression! — by his presence.

He had begun to speak, and she, occupied only with herself, heard him without understanding, without taking account of what he said. He was pleading for someone, for indulgence and forbearance; he did it in his forceful, captivating way. Probably no one else had ever heard him plead so warmly, so gently, so modestly. There was nothing on earth more insinuating than the sound of his voice. The name that came again and again to his lips was Alma's.

Suddenly Maria roused herself from her difficult struggle. "What exactly do you want?" she asked harshly. "What should I do for Alma?"

"What I beg of you."

"And that is?"

"Oh — you don't even give me as much attention as you would any beggar who spoke to you on the street," Tessin cried reproachfully. "What are you thinking of? Always only of that happy man who through you has become the first among men. Yes, yes, yes! He who may boast of possessing the most precious of worldly goods, a woman like you, is the first among men."

"He does not boast," she objected.

Tessin laughed. "It would be only human — and he has the obligation to be perfection itself, and he meets that obligation. But another man, too, a lesser man, who had had his luck, would have known how to make himself worthy of it . . . . Countess, Countess! I believe that, at your side, even I could have become not only good, but a champion of what is good."

Maria bent over her work and said, "One does good for the sake of good itself. When it is done for another reason it is worthless."

"You deny conversion brought about by saints, by prophets," countered Tessin, "the overwhelming power of example? I do not belong to the chosen few who draw water from the fountainhead. I require the hand of a friend who is generous enough to do it for me and then to impart to me something of its glorious refreshment. Man's benefactor is always man alone. I would give all the divine protection and the so-called rule and providence of an infinite wisdom for the constancy of a heart that loved me, and I would be enviable indeed were it in my power to make that exchange. Countess," he began again, after a short silence, "as unimportant as I am to you, perhaps you nevertheless noticed that a great change took place in me in the short, happy time in which I ventured to raise my eyes to you . . . . So full of reverence, so humble, and — so foolishly bold . . . . Oh, if I were still able to blush, I would have to at this confession" — and a dark flush stained his face — "for I had hoped to win you. A childishly bold venture, striving for such a goal. A relative of Alma Tessin would not be permitted to become the son-in-law of Count Wolfsberg. I should have known that and have been prepared for what happened."

"What happened . . . ." she repeated tonelessly.

"I was stricken from the ranks of your suitors — "

"My suitors? You had asked for my hand?"

"You didn't know that? Your father didn't tell you!" cried Tessin with bitterness and sarcasm. "So that's the strategy of a Wolfsberg — neither candid nor fair, but clever. Why present you with a choice when he has decided not to allow you to choose? You had already been disposed of; before you had any idea of it, you had been promised to Count Dornach."

"Promised?" cried Maria indignantly.

"Let us say, rather, intended. Your father simply brushed me aside after I had been uprooted in your good opinion . . . thanks to him — please, don't deny it — thanks to him. I won't ask how he accomplished that. The life of a man of the world, whose vocation it is to follow every fashion, offers many a weak point. And I wear no suit of armor. Any arrow aimed at me will pierce my unprotected breast. But you, Countess, so wise, so just, so high-minded, you could not find a single excuse for me, not a single charitable thought. You turned away, silent and contemptuous — I will never forget the manner in which you turned away from me!"

She was shaken by his accusation; she looked at him and said, losing all presence of mind, "You, too, were silent — if you had only spoken then. Now it is too late."

"Spoken to *you*?" he asked quickly, ignoring her last words, "To you, in whose heart nothing spoke for me? Nothing. Otherwise you would not have given me up so easily. He who is scorned does not always wish to justify himself. He is easily hurt; he is sensitive. No, I wanted to wait until I could wish you well at the same time and at least prove my unselfishness. Absurd, wasn't it? It was ridiculous. One foolish act followed another . . . . To be sure, I would have handled it all differently if I had not been so unfortunate as to — love you."

What could she say? In her heart she acknowledged that he was right. He had never practiced his seductive arts on her. This man, about whom it was said that he never courted a woman in vain, that he was never forgotten by those he abandoned, had never been other than modest, almost shy, in her presence. She could not contradict him as he began again, "Tell me, could a schoolboy have behaved more awkwardly, more stupidly in the presence of the woman he silently, though ardently adored than I have behaved toward you? Finished! My 'pleasure-filled' life is empty; it is nothing. Now I am going to try my hand at ambition," he continued with a deep sigh, "the solution of many a man run aground. If you hear one day that I have 'become' something that seems worthwhile, then remember this hour and weigh the significance that any outward glory in life could possibly have for me."

He stopped. He waited. Maria was silent. Almost timidly, Tessin returned after a while to his first request, speaking again of Alma.

"Have sympathy with an unhappy woman, a little sympathy, Countess. She herself does not dare to beseech you. She does not feel that she is even allowed to live in the same city with you; she buries herself and pines away with loneliness and remorse in the country — "

"She does right," Maria interrupted him, coldly and quietly. "How did she have the audacity to associate with me previously and with — it is inconceivable — a hundred others who all knew of her guilt, which is beyond atonement?"

"Beyond atonement? I believe she does atone for it."

"Let her try." With that she rose, and he leapt to his feet.

"You are dismissing me?"

"Farewell."

"Your hand! Give me your hand in farewell. Duelists shake hands when one has disarmed the other. Countess Maria, I have experienced the cruelest defeat. I have lost everything — hope, courage, strength. You have even broken the wretched pride that still maintained me. Give me your hand out of pity!" He gnashed his teeth; his noble, proud face was deathly pale.

Maria shook her head.

After a last questioning, pleading look he bowed and left the room.

Maria followed him with her eyes. She had indeed won a complete victory over herself; for truly, the pity he had begged of her filled her breast almost to the point of bursting, and it would have been sweet bliss to take the hand he stretched out to her in parting and to say, "You do not suffer alone. Take that consolation with you."

But she had not been able to give him her hand. He would have felt how it trembled and was icy, because all the blood in her body rushed to her rebellious heart, which pounded so madly in response.

*   *   *

Shortly before the train departed, Hermann and Maria arrived at the station, and a few minutes later the locomotive steamed out of the station hall.

"Isn't that Tessin?" Hermann asked, pointing to a dark figure that stood in the shadow of a pillar and watched the wagon as it pulled away.

Maria had long since seen him. "Yes, it is Tessin."

"Looking like someone who is about to kill himself," Hermann responded. "I find him so uncanny lately."

It was another warm, beautiful spring night like the one two years ago on which they had begun their wedding trip to Dornach. Maria pressed herself into a corner and closed her eyes, and again, when she looked up, she encountered her husband's gaze resting lovingly upon her.

He had noticed immediately that she was upset. He attributed it to the hasty departure that had put a sudden end to the pleasures offered by the city, pleasures that were particularly abundant just now. He found it understandable and regretted having accepted Maria's sacrifice and having allowed her to accompany him to Dornachtal.

"If we can safely leave my mother," he said, "we'll go back to Vienna for the races in May."

Maria objected, "We don't want to do that; you are not interested, and I — believe me — I long for the tranquillity of Dornach. We want to go there as soon as your mother no longer needs us. To Dornach, dear — there everything will be all right again." She had spoken these last words involuntarily, more to herself than to him, and not with conviction, but with anguished uncertainty.

Hermann seized her hands. "What will be all right *again*? What is not all right? Speak, tell me, my everything, my child and my deity. My benefactress! What is keeping *you* from being happy?"

She pulled her hands away in order to place them on his shoulders and looked deeply into his peaceful eyes. "My friend . . . my friend," she repeated and thought about confessing everything to him, about saying to him, "Help

51

me — liberate me — I am struggling in terrible shackles. It gnaws at my heart; it is a wicked sympathy — a criminal longing. Help, help, save me from the confusion I have fallen into!"

Should she say that to him?

It lasted a moment, and then she was amazed that it could have occurred to her at all. Wasn't all danger past? What was left to fight against? Just a storm of emotions that she wanted to master on her own.

"Nothing," she said. "It was only a mood, dearest, to which all mortals are subject, with the sole exception of you. I can only repeat what I said to you when we were engaged: have patience with me."

* * *

Countess Agathe received her children, when they arrived the next day shortly before lunch, with a deliberate display of surprise. She was indeed still in bed, but only out of consideration for the exaggerated anxiety of her physician. It was very unpleasant for her, she asserted, to know that the little one was alone at Dornach — and on her account. She brooked no objection and insisted, "Such a young child is always alone without his mother. Do not worry about me! What the Lord wills, we must humbly accept. But I hope that He will be merciful, that He will hear my prayer and leave me here to bless my third grandson. There must be three. One for Dornach, one for God, one for the emperor."

"Heir, priest, soldier," murmured Father Schirmer, nodded three times, folded his small hands over his stomach, and peered out of his tiny eyes, over the plump cushions of his cheeks, with a wealth of goodwill and kindness.

The countess was appeased only when Maria had sent a telegram to Dornach announcing her arrival three evenings hence. Hermann was asked to stay longer. That was at the suggestion of Father Schirmer, who, entrusted with the office of secretary, had tolerated ruinous carelessness in the management of business affairs as a consequence of his aspiration to "avoid any disruption of the harmony between the property owner and its steward." With alarm he had become aware of the mischief his weakness had caused. The intervention of Hermann's firm hand was necessary.

Maria, therefore, arrived at Dornach alone.

Wilhelm was waiting at the station and received his cousin with as much emotion as a lover. He repeated the welcoming babble of his "splendid nephew," Helmi's warmest regards, and the scamps' respectful greetings. He was able to confirm the written reports on Wolf Forster's condition that Dr. Weise had sent to Vienna over the course of the winter. The patient was well enough to leave Dornach and to make the trip to Hermann's hunting grounds in the Tyrol. Hermann had granted him a permanent residence in the hunting lodge there. He himself was very happy about the prospect and now spoke only of his long-cherished and only reluctantly subdued "passion" for hunting.

52

"Nothing but good, dear Wilhelm — you bring nothing but good news," said Maria, and tears welled up in her eyes.

"You bring the best thing, Countess," he cried. "You bring *yourself*."

"What did you say? Countess?"

"I beg your pardon! It's because of my respect . . . . After such a long separation, it seems downright impudent to me . . . ." He was embarrassed and fell silent.

They rolled forward with the quick trot of the horses.

The sky arched over them transparently blue and cloudless. To the west, in a low point of the mountain ridges, the setting sun formed a dazzling ball of fire and sent its rays of greeting out over the budding, sprouting, blossoming world that it had awakened to new life.

Eternally solved, eternally insoluble mystery, miracle of spring! Maria quietly allowed it to act upon her and worshipped the one and only power that moves and sprouts in the blade of grass in the meadow, echoes from the resonant breast of the nightingale, tempts and strives irresistibly within the human heart.

They had arrived at the manor house; Wilhelm mounted his horse and rode home, after promising to appear at Dornach the next day as "paterfamilias."

Maria held her child in her arms; she kissed and caressed him and repeated her motto: "Everything is all right; everything is fine."

Oh, if only she did not have to reproach herself — bitterly, repeatedly, agonizingly — for having been mercilessly cruel to someone who had not wronged her, no, someone whom *she* had wronged. She should have conquered herself, should have given him her hand and said — what prevented her from doing so, what duty forbade her? — "I loved you. Long ago, when I was still free. Circumstances have separated us. Now, like good people, we want to do our duty and to meet as old friends when we see each other again years from now, after the feelings that now oppress and confuse us have been extinguished."

If she had only said this, had only been able to say this! Weakness, weakness, not to have been able to. Now the sting remained in her breast, the drop of poison in her blood. She would never forget the look he had cast her as he left.

When Maria had gone to her bedroom, Lisette appeared to say good night and to bring her a message from Forster. "He is leaving," she said, "and he entreats you to play the piano tomorrow and then to come to the summerhouse. He would like so much to bid you farewell and also to spare you the long walk to the house of the forester's widow. Will you come?"

"Yes."

"Something else. Just imagine. Today he had a visitor, Wolfi did. A friend of his, who is making a long journey, stopped here between trains."

Maria pushed the screen, which stood on the table, in front of the lamp. "Who?" she asked.

"I don't know his name. Such a tall, handsome man; the face of an Italian. He had side-whiskers, coal-black, somewhat curly hair, a Roman nose, a clean-shaven chin. Perhaps you know him, although I never saw him at our house."

After the old woman had left, Maria wandered for a long time through the room and thought of the one whom every minute, every second carried further away from her and who was probably also awake and suffered as she did and thought of her with resentment and anger . . . .

He had been here; he had wanted to take with him into his voluntary exile the memory of the place where she lived. Just one day — just one, and they would have seen each other and been able to part in the way that she pictured to herself in ever lovelier, ever purer colors.

Morning came. Holding his nurse's hand, her little child tottered, reckless and unsteady, into the bedroom and to his mother's bed, shouting with joy.

Maria rose after a few brief hours of uncomfortable sleep that had been disturbed by desolate dreams. She wanted to begin the day's work, but she seemed to have lead in all her limbs and an iron band around her head. Everything was difficult, everything failed her, even her faithful art. She closed the piano after striking a few chords, hurried outside, walked around the house, and wandered down a lilac path toward the summerhouse. Forster was waiting for her there; she wanted to meet him and to hear news of the man who had left from the last person to speak to him in his native land.

She had arrived and crossed the steps that led to the little entrance of the small structure, a delicate and luxurious trifle from the eighteenth century. It had two rooms separated by Roman arches. The walls and the furniture were covered with yellow Chinese silk, and the windows were hung with the same costly fabric.

As Maria stepped out of the brilliant sunshine into this golden twilight, her eyes were dazzled and she was unable to distinguish any clear outlines. From the adjacent room someone approached, it seemed to her, slowly and with hesitation. "Forster," she called.

No answer. Only after a moment did she hear her softly whispered name.

Maria recognized the voice immediately and cried out, "You!"

Tessin rushed toward her, his hands clasped in fervent entreaty. She extended hers to fend him off.

"Away! How dare you? This is treachery. Go!"

He shook his head. "Not like this. I have tried — it is impossible." Determination in every movement, his brows drawn together threateningly, he came closer.

She retreated in silence and moved toward the entrance.

Then he threw himself between her and the door, and, as Maria ran to the nearest window and attempted to open it with trembling fingers that failed to obey her, a grim smile crept over his features.

"You want to call for help — do it. I must yield to force. But not alive . . . . I promise you that — and you," he raised his right hand solemnly, "you believe me."

"Madness!" stammered Maria, trembling with fear and consternation.

"No, despair! What have I done to you? Why do you despise me? I have loved you beyond expression. And what have you done to me? You have scorned me, mistreated me, as I allow no one to mistreat me. You have failed to recognize the purest sentiment of my life, have attributed base motives to me, have coldly and calculatingly wounded me in the most sensitive place in my heart — I demand satisfaction!" He looked at her, agitated, in mad excitement. But suddenly, as though cast under a calming spell, he sank to one knee.

What had happened?

A woman, tormented by fear, struggling with tears, stood before him. Her pride was broken; in a weak voice, she said, "You must go."

"Yes, yes!" He grasped her resisting hand. "On one condition . . . . Give me that sign of pity I begged of you before. I will receive as a favor what should be my right, what you owe me, for everything . . . also for the murder of that better man who slumbered within me, who wished to awaken under your influence, and whom you killed when you gave me up."

He assailed her more and more fervently; his speech flowed more and more convincingly; an intoxicating breath of passion emanated from him. "What is it that I ask, after all? One word of comfort to carry with me, one kind look, one touch of your hand . . . ."

That she could give him; it was what she had been longing for — a farewell in peace and reconciliation before parting forever.

His eyes flashed up to hers. She bent down, she looked into his eyes, and she whispered, "Because this is our last meeting, Tessin . . . you must know . . . I did not give you up easily . . . I was not indifferent to you . . . ."

Here he broke into a joyous cry: "At last! At last!" Softly and tenderly, in blissful gratitude, he pressed his forehead, his lips to her hand, and Maria, struggling in this most difficult battle, whispered softly to him, "Now go."

Completely transformed, beside himself, he sprang to his feet. "No! No! You loved me; you love me still!" He pulled her into his arms and with his kisses smothered the cry she uttered.

She wanted to pull herself away from him — she wanted to save herself — and lay on his breast, irresistibly drawn to him as though by the force of nature.

Two ecstatic people had lost all consciousness of honor, duty, and fidelity; for them the world and all memory had disappeared.

* * *

The sun was at its zenith; Maria was alone.

For a long time, for a very long time — for an eternity . . . . Or not? Had she only just been left alone upon waking out of a horrible, blissful, impossible ecstasy?

She sat there, her hands on the table, her face buried in her hands, as the door opened and a wheezing, gasping breathing became audible.

Wolfi dragged himself in, leaning on a cane, and fell heavily on the sofa next to Maria. He stretched out his legs, leaned back, and groaned, "That's it for me. I'll have to pay dearly for that bit of fun."

Maria stared at him, horrified by his appearance. He looked as though he were dying. "You're exhausted; the walk here was too much for you," she said.

"The walk here?" He wanted to laugh, but only a sort of sob emerged from his throat. "No, it was having to lead your lover through the forest — so he wouldn't get lost. And then his gratitude — he threatened to run me through because I didn't want to swear to keep quiet. Swear to *him*, to a man without honor."

Maria was thunderstruck. She had been lured into a trap. Tessin had had a confidant. Had needed one. Of course — in order to find opportunities, one needs people to create them, assistants, accomplices. Someone like that base fellow there . . . . Her heart stood still as these thoughts shot through her, cold and clear. Will death come? Oh, if only it would come of its own accord, so that she would not have to seek it — because how could she go on living now?

"Tired . . . I'm so tired," Wolfi groaned. "I can't get comfortable. Help me a little."

Overcome with disgust and loathing, Maria struggled with herself but then bent over; Wolfi put his arms around her neck, she took him by the shoulders, laid him — he seemed as light as a child to her — lengthwise on the sofa, and pushed pillows under his head. "Don't move. I'll send the doctor."

"Don't need him — not him — just you — I'm already better . . . . Your care does me good — If you had always been kind to me — perhaps I would have spared you — perhaps . . . . One can't say for sure — a man like me . . . ." He stopped. His breathing grew still more labored. The red spots on his cheeks grew darker. Now his features altered strangely; suddenly they assumed a gentle, almost noble expression.

"You are no longer proud," he said, almost inaudibly. "You no longer despise anyone?"

She, with heartrending lament, answered, "Myself!"

"Will you now call me brother?"

"Brother."

"Victory!" His remaining strength was exhausted by the effort with which he produced this word. A stream of blood gushed from his mouth; his head, which he had raised slightly, sank back into the pillows.

Maria uttered a cry of horror. "Help! Help! He is dying!"

XI.

The cries for help that came from the summerhouse were heard first by the child of a laborer; the child did not venture nearer but summoned others. Servants ran for the doctor. When he came he found the countess in a blood-spattered dress, collapsed, half-unconscious, beside Wolfi's body. She could not be persuaded to leave until every possible attempt to revive him had been made.

As Dr. Weise had predicted, all was in vain. He allowed himself to quote the declaration he had often made to Miss Lisette: becoming severely overheated or something similar, or having one of the attacks of rage to which Mr. Forster was subject, and during which he tended to scream as though possessed, could cause a blood vessel to burst; however, he might have lived to be an old man had he only resolved to behave like one now. The laughter with which the patient used to respond to this prognosis had always annoyed the doctor.

"And it still annoys me," he said to Wilhelm and his wife, whom he met on the road after driving out in his buggy in the afternoon in order to tell them first of the sad event at Dornach and of the circumstances under which it had taken place. He also asked them to decide whether or not the count should be summoned by telegram out of concern for the countess, who, as a consequence of the shock she had endured, was in a state of great agitation.

"Very upset, although making an effort to exercise self-control. I checked her pulse without her noticing — it could hardly be counted. I wouldn't be surprised if something develops," he said, with the traditional doctor's shake of the head.

"If *what* develops?" Wilhelm asked, jumping out of the carriage in the greatest dismay, seizing the doctor's arm, and looking up at him anxiously.

"Well, now," replied the latter with an expression of importance, "a slight case of typhoid fever, or an inflammation — *cordis basis* — *cordis conus* . . . ."[14]

"Is that dangerous? The devil take these names that no one understands, that only make you worry," he said, turning to his wife. She had also gotten out of the carriage, had come to his side, and attempted to comfort him.

"Calm yourself; it won't be so serious. But we must send the boys home," she said.

"Certainly," and Wilhelm surveyed the heads of his dear ones, who peered out of the roomy hunting wagon as though from a pen. "If there were only two or three of them, it would still be all right. But eight at such a time — impossible. Drive them home," he said to the old coachman, who possessed his complete confidence because he had ten children himself.

The revolution that threatened to break out in the carriage was quelled by a few commanding words from the father and the gentle remonstrance of the mother. Willi, the oldest, received permission to sit on the box and drive; the others were left to their disappointment.

Wilhelmine did not accept the seat the doctor offered her beside him in his "shell on wheels." An ever faithful companion, she walked toward the castle at the side of her deeply worried spouse. In the hall they met Lisette. She was searching for the doctor; today, for the first time, she did not quite understand him. How could he leave the house during Maria's worrisome indisposition and neglect such an excellent opportunity to make himself indispensable? And where was he now?

"He drove to the village," Wilhelm answered and hurried up the stairs.

His wife followed him and had difficulty persuading him to wait in the drawing room until she could tell him whether their cousin could see him.

Maria was in her bedroom, where she had been pacing for hours, restlessly, with hurried steps. At Wilhelmine's quiet knock, she stood still and, after the former had identified herself, cried, "Come in, come in! I have been longing to see you."

"Here I am, and I will stay with you until you are calmer, poor, poor child!" She took her hand, pressed it lovingly, and struggled against the sympathy and the pain that almost overwhelmed her at the sight of the devastation and despair in Maria's face.

Her motherly tenderness and persuasiveness were finally successful in prevailing upon the exhausted woman to sit down in an armchair and even to take a little nourishment.

"The man who died today was my brother," Maria said suddenly. "Did you know that?"

Wilhelmine answered simply, "Certainly; no secret was made of it."

"And I was unfeeling and arrogant toward him, do you understand? Me!" She burst into tears. She sobbed. The terrible tension of her soul had relaxed.

Gradually she regained control of herself, asked to see Wilhelm, and became only for a moment violently agitated when he made the suggestion that Hermann be sent a telegram.

"Under no circumstances! He would come."

"And should he not?"

"No, his mother needs him. I will write to him," she added hastily. "You can depend on me. No one else is to write him. Give me your word."

"What a woman!" Wilhelmine said to her husband as they drove home. "She proves to me anew that the truly noble and good can never do enough to be satisfied with themselves. Were not extraordinary measures taken for the unfortunate Forster? And even now Maria still reproaches herself. Such things are the measure of a soul's worth. What a woman! I have taken her into my heart as though she were my ninth child."

Maria's letter to Hermann must have been written with composure and deliberation; the detailed telegram that Wilhelm received from his cousin the following evening did not express the least anxiety about Maria. Hermann asked

Wilhelm to make arrangements for a dignified burial and hoped to be able to return to Dornach at the end of the next week.

Forster's body had hardly been consigned to the earth when all sorts of rumors surfaced about the immediate cause of his death. A hunter alleged that he had seen him shortly beforehand near the edge of the forest on a path that led to the north train station. He was arguing with a tall, dark-haired man, whom the hunter, from a distance, had taken for the assistant steward. The assistant steward was called to account but was able to prove easily that he, on that day and at that hour, had been in the neighboring town where the head forester had sent him to buy grass seed. Obviously the hunter was mistaken about the identity of the individual with whom Wolfi had recently associated to his detriment. No one doubted that there had been such a person.

"It could have been," said the doctor, with his usual circumspection, "a smuggler, through whom my patient wanted perhaps to obtain cigars behind my back. Or perhaps a creditor, who made an attempt to collect his money."

Lisette, on the other hand, declared that she was convinced that it was the same swindler who — she had noticed something suspicious about him immediately — had visited the "poor, dear boy" quite openly the day before and then, heaven knows why, might have returned in secret. Even so, however, the situation was still far from clear. And despite all inquiries, the mystery of the stranger's identity and his relationship to Forster remained unsolved.

Maria had wrapped herself in a resignation verging on indifference. Let them discover the truth! She would not deny it; she would die. With presumptuous confidence, she trusted in the compassion of the All-merciful. He would allow her to perish of her feelings of guilt, allow her to do penance, allow her to atone through death. It was a comfort to her to repeat that to herself. One certainly cannot live with feelings of shame like those she carried within her. Something awaited her, something inconceivable, unimaginable — the reunion with her husband. She will not be able to endure his gaze; she will receive him with a confession. "I have betrayed you once, in a cursed hour, in vile delirium. But to betray you again, consciously and deliberately, to offer my desecrated mouth to be kissed — that I will never do."

He came and was inexpressibly happy to be there again, and she stood motionless before him — and was silent.

Like the others, he attributed her wretched appearance, her melancholy mood, to the terrible impression Wolfi's death had made on her. The doctor congratulated him on the accuracy of this view, using many foreign words, as befits a country doctor who is treating a distinguished patient.

Miss Lisette acquired something dignified and victorious in her gait and her gestures at about that time. Her heart, which had never known a more ardent attachment than that to "her child," asserted its vernal rights in late autumn. She loved and she flattered herself that she was loved; her thoughts flocked around the precious object, and only here and there did a few of them descend on the one she had once worshipped and adored exclusively. Lisette found it unnecessary to conceal her passion and spoke openly of the one who inspired it in her.

"His name is always on my lips," she said once in a mischievous tone to her mistress, skillfully inserting a remark about the doctor into the middle of a report on the arrival of a shipment of table linen.

"Whose name?" asked Maria.

And now the elderly spinster made her confession, long since proclaimed. Maria listened at first with negligible and then with growing attention, and suddenly something extraordinary happened — Maria laughed.

Hermann, who was just entering, heard it and burst into exultation. "Who made you laugh? You, Lisette? Precious Lisette! What should I do for you? I will establish a foundation for ladies of the bedchamber, and you shall be its sovereign ruler." He rushed to her and kissed her resoundingly on each cheek. "What did she say to you?" he asked, turning to his wife, and pushed a chair next to the sofa where she sat and seated himself. "I want to know; I want to take lessons from her."

Maria asked, "May I answer, Lisette?" and the latter, a little shamefaced, responded, "If you please."

"With your permission, then. She would like to marry the doctor."

Hermann's bewilderment, the effort he made to conceal it, the cheerful, infinite goodness that shone from his eyes and in the irrepressible and innocent smile that played around his mouth, elicited Maria's merriment anew.

So was it possible, still — even so soon — could something lift her out of the oppressive, justified, requisite agony of her soul?

One night she lay awake, as she often did, listened to the peaceful breathing of her husband, and thought and thought.

And now a hoarse sound, an audible, ragged coughing from a tiny chest, reached her ear out of the silence of the adjacent room where the child slept. She rose quietly, threw on her dressing gown, glided over the carpet with bare feet, her slippers in her hand, entered the child's room, and pushed back the curtain around his little bed. The light of the night lamp fell on the flushed face of the little boy; he was moaning heavily in feverish sleep. Maria woke him and his nurse and administered a simple remedy, while the nurse, on Maria's orders, roused the nurserymaid and sent a servant for the doctor. He came, said nothing, but took action calmly and with determination; he was a model of courage and presence of mind that night. Only temporarily did he fly into a rage at the nurse, who rushed around, beside herself, and insisted that the count should be called.

"Foolish woman!" cried Weise, forsaking the politeness that otherwise characterized him. "The doctor forbids it, the doctor does not need frightened people in the sickroom. There, now that's composure. That's the right behavior — take that as your example." He pointed to Maria, who held the child on her lap.

Deathly pale in her snow-white robes, she watched unwaveringly every change in the boy's condition, advised the doctor of each one, and carried out all of his orders herself, holding a mute conversation with her child. "Do you want to go on before me, to wait for me there? I will follow you soon. But your poor father! Is he to lose both at the same time? A genuine treasure — you — and another that is worthless and false, but which he will mourn in his untroubled faith as though it had truly been a precious possession. Stay with him, my darling; offer him the richest compensation." She pressed him to her breast, and he fixed his large eyes on her and murmured, "Dear Mama."

"He is better, isn't he, Doctor?" asked Maria.

"Unless all the signs mislead us," he answered.

She understood him. He had returned to his conditional statements. The anxiety that had led him to abandon his customary pedantic caution had dissipated.

Only in the morning did Hermann discover that his little son had been dangerously ill and that he had been saved.

"Saved for you," thought Maria, "for your consolation when I am no longer with you." She had made up her mind. God had left her prayers unanswered, had consigned her to despair; she therefore made a desperate decision.

A beautiful path through the woods led to the ruins of an ancient fortified castle that crowned the rocky summit of a mountain covered to more than half its height with silver firs. On the opposite side, however, one could reach the ruin by a much shorter path. This one went over a narrow footbridge that had no railing and led to the bottom of a steep precipice, not far from a half-crumbled flight of steps hewn in the rock. A daring and skillful climber might use these steps to reach the summit; that is, if he did not become dizzy. Otherwise, a backward look into the gorge might prove fatal. The same stream that, a few hundred steps further, flowed peacefully through the meadows, navigated there by rowboats, became a torrent in this narrow ravine. Seething and roaring, the spraying current circled and formed deep whirlpools, turned round and round, rose in pillars of foam, then madly threw itself back into its rocky bed, luring the onlooker to participation in its gushing, inexhaustible high spirits.

In her first year of marriage, Maria had visited the ruins. Overcome by a stirring of that untameable delight in danger that had often seized her in her early youth, she had climbed down the rocky steps and crossed the footbridge with a firm and certain gait.

Hermann, to whom she had confessed her daring feat, could only be appeased by her solemn vow never to repeat it. Now that promise must be broken.

With meticulous and inventive precision, Maria pictured it all to herself, saw herself step onto the bridge and move forward and then slowly and deliberately slip at just the right spot . . . totter, fall, be shattered on the rocks that, always shining, always wetly glistening, projected from the water. She imagined Hermann's grief — it would be tinged with anger — and that was only right. Guilty as she was, she did not deserve to leave behind an unsullied memory.

She prepared herself for the terrible parting from her small child, who still needed his mother so much; she took leave of him day after day. "Tomorrow it will happen," she would say to herself, until the day came when she realized that she could not die without committing a double murder.

And that she could not do. To be sure, a thought flamed up inside her: Bury the fruit of transgression with you! But to *kill* in order to atone? She was still pious and devout, and she asked in her agony of soul, "How would You receive the murderer of a child, Eternal Judge, Lord, my God?"

Woman's most powerful instinct raised its mighty voice within her . . . . Perhaps, without her knowledge, the life force, now doubled, struggled against annihilation.

She returned to the solution that had at first seemed to be the obvious one, the only one: to confess everything to Hermann, to tell him, "*This is what I am*; treat me as I deserve. I can no longer endure your goodness, I yearn for punishment, for penance. The more severe, the better; grant me this, grant me the comfort of penance. Be merciless; only adore me no longer."

And while she spoke thus in her thoughts, reason responded, "Words, empty words! You know he will never cast you out, never expose you to scorn; even if you were to kill his happiness, he would not place his foot upon your neck, fallen though you are. He will remain unshaken in his forbearance. Separated, inwardly estranged from you, he will still demand respect for you from others. Then you will have taken on a new burden of gratitude and destroyed in vain the best of all that fills his heart and elevates his soul. You have nothing to lose, while he will lose everything. You will have made him miserable to no purpose — you *must* not do it!"

All that had transpired earlier paled in comparison to what she did now. She carried out the deception that was to conceal the disgrace. Hermann must be deceived. It was so easy and therefore so wicked . . . and yet it was done. And Maria endured the degradation she had considered inconceivable — all of it. She was spared nothing — not the joy with which her duped husband received the news she stammered in the darkness of night, not his increased tenderness, not Wilhelm's good-natured jokes, not Helmi's warm concern, not Countess Agathe's solemn good wishes.

Maria acted a wretched part, pretended interest in indifferent things, enjoyment in harmless pleasures, in the excursions and outdoor parties that Hermann and Wilhelm organized in order to amuse her. Hermann usually, but not always, allowed himself to be deceived. All his happiness was based on the picture he had formed of hers.

She, on the other hand, lived in her love for her child, zealously practiced her art, which she performed more beautifully and more enchantingly than ever before, and gradually arrived at a peculiar form of sophistry. The atonement she longed for lay certainly in the realization that she was unable to atone. Fate's decree for her was this: "You love truth; now live a lie."

XII.

In the summer Count Wolfsberg and his sister, with her companion, Miss Annette Ninnemann, came to Dornach. Almost on their heels, without being invited, without announcing her visit, the little Countess Felicitas Soltan followed. She came in order to ask whether Tessin, as he had promised before his departure, had written to Countess Dolph, and how he was, and especially — whether he had sent greetings to her.

However, no letter from him had yet arrived, and only through newspaper telegrams had they learned that he had arrived at his post and had been ceremoniously received.

On a humid Sunday afternoon the manor's inhabitants had assembled in a large, open tent on the bank of the pond. Dense shrubbery surrounded them on all sides, and behind that the pale green picturesque branches of individual tulip trees and, at greater distance, the dark treetops of a pine grove rose into the uniform, tranquilly luminous blue of the sky.

All those present in the tent, with the exception of Miss Ninnemann and Hermann junior, were smoking. Annette had pushed her chair closer and closer to the entrance, but malicious[15] tobacco smoke floated after her and made her cough a little, which Countess Dolph censured vigorously. She sat far back in the tent in a padded beach chair and wore a cap that was remarkably reminiscent of the domestic headgear of French kings in the fifteenth century.

"Ninny," she said.

"My name is Ninnemann," corrected the companion, without turning around.

"Well, then, Ninnemann, don't force yourself to cough — out of sheer affectation."

Annette shrugged her shoulders and pressed the palms of her damp hands together; her red, protruding lips displayed their characteristic nervous quivering.

Fée nodded to her sympathetically and sighed, "Oh, what heat! Is it always so hot here, Count Dornach?" She rocked herself in her rocking chair, her eyes were half-closed, and she let her arms dangle beside her slender and delicate body as though she were completely exhausted.

Count Wolfsberg, whom she had made up her mind to amuse, was an ungrateful audience today. He had not even noticed that she was wearing his favorite dress, the white embroidered one with the pink baby's bow. At the table, where she, only in order to entertain him, had revealed all of the most hallowed secrets of her heart, had spoken of her unpaid bills, of her belief in the future of spiritualism as the state religion, of any number of her ethical considerations — intimate, extremely intimate things! — he had hardly listened. And now he had been sitting silently and solemnly next to her for an hour, and she had finally given up hope of extricating him from his ill humor.

Hermann and Maria knew the reason for his dark mood. He had gone to the cemetery while the others were in church and had visited Wolfi's grave.

"What for? Why does he do such things, when they upset him far too much?" Dolph had complained to her niece. She, too, tried to distract him and attempted to enlist the most effective support, that of little Hermann, but it was not to be had at the moment. The little boy had collected small stones and laid them in his mother's lap and, with her help, was now industriously throwing them into the water. His response to his great aunt's invitation to come to her was a decided negative, and the frankest aversion was expressed in the quick glance he cast up at the old woman.

Countess Dolph vented the annoyance she felt at the futility of the affection-ate efforts she had long lavished on this beautiful and charming child, by sud-denly speaking of the disagreeable things she associated with life in the country.

"One appalling thing, for instance," she said, "is that one's attendance at church is scrutinized. One cannot miss a single service, and I tell you, one more high mass like the one today and you can just keep me there in your family crypt. And you, Ninny, I insist that you do not seat yourself in the oratory across from us next Sunday. You disturb me; you rob me of the last bit of devo-tion I still possess, with your mixture of exaltation and fits of nausea."

This attack was repelled by Miss Annette with unaccustomed composure. When the devotion of one must suffer as the result of another's, she said, then let it be the inferior devotion — that of the countess.

Fée applauded and assured her that she was the cleverest Ninnemann ever to walk the earth; then the tiny woman, with Hermann's assistance, climbed into the boat moored to the bank. It must not be cast off. She wanted to stay there, to rock herself in the cool water, and to hear how Count Wolfsberg's conversation sounded *from a distance.*

He finally condescended to call out a jest to her, to which she responded as readily as she did inappropriately. The ensuing battle between them, conducted with animation on her side, was interrupted by the arrival of the mail.

Maria distributed the newspapers and the letters.

"Is there something for me?" "For me?" asked Fée and Countess Dolph.

"Yes." Maria pushed a thick letter toward the latter.

"From Tessin," said the countess. "From Tessin," she repeated louder and waved the letter in the air. "Fée, look here."

"For Fée," Maria said, and Hermann took from her hands an entire shipment of fashion magazines and newspapers, which he transferred to the boat.

"Those are your unpaid bills," cried Wolfsberg. "Be careful, Countess, your vessel is sinking under their weight."

At Tessin's name, Felicitas had jumped up so quickly that her small vessel began to rock in an alarming manner. She fell back, screamed, and threw herself so violently from side to side that it seemed as though she intended to upset the boat entirely.

Hermann pulled it close to shore broadside and said, half laughing, half an-noyed, "Your life is saved; come ashore."

The high-spirited woman resisted. "Not yet! Not yet! I want someone to write to Tessin that I almost drowned for joy when I heard that a letter from him had arrived. You are a witness, Miss Ninnemann; swear to it. I want a regular oath — please!"

"Oh no, Countess, I can't make jokes about such sacred things," the com-panion reproached her.

"No? Oh dear! Then you must swear, Count Wolfsberg."

The count answered mechanically, "Yes, yes." His entire attention was fo-cused on Maria.

She had laid a letter on the table in front of her, a second letter from Tessin, even thicker and heavier than the one addressed to Countess Dolph, and had sunk into contemplation of the strong, easy handwriting of the address. Rigid horror was reflected in her face. If these few lines had announced death and de-struction, she would have looked down at them in just this way.

She seemed to sense that her father's eyes rested upon her, raised hers, looked at him — and bowed her head slowly.

This brief, mute conversation between father and daughter was observed by no one. Countess Dolph luxuriated in the enjoyment of the witty epistle from her Horace Walpole; Miss Ninnemann followed the spectacle of Fée's "rescue" by Hermann with interest. Despite all the antics of its heroine, it had a happy end-ing.

Hermann came into the tent, stopped behind Maria's chair, and, looking over her shoulder, read the name of the recipient of Tessin's second letter: "Mr. Wolfgang Forster."

A discussion ensued as to what should be done with the letter.

"It's so thick," said Fée, "there are surely a few others inside, which Mr. For-ster was to have passed on. We must open it."

Countess Dolph endorsed that. "We must open it, certainly."

Hermann, however, declared that it did not seem at all so "certain" to him. "What do you think, Maria?" he asked and passed his hand over her hair.

She turned, seized this hand, and pressed it to her lips. That was enough to arouse the jealousy of little Hermann toward big Hermann. The child cried and reached up to her, and she lifted him onto her knee and pressed her face against his.

She still had him; she still had a love whose whole value she had begun to recognize after she had made herself unworthy of it — the love of the best of men. She still had the esteem of all good people . . . . Just a short while, just a tear through the thin paper wrapping there on the table — and everything will be over, and the hell of disgrace will open before her.

Her little boy puts his arms around her neck, and she puts hers around him. But this most sacred embrace does not protect her. She does not hear the affectionate whispering of the sweet childish voice — she hears another, dreadful one, which calls to her, "Why do you shudder? Certainly not because of what will follow the truth, for which you have longed and yearned. Here it is — welcome it. Do it, wretched one . . . . Or was it, after all, something other than deception that you have dreaded most? Where is your loathing of it now?" "I still feel it," thought Maria, kissed the child, and put him on the ground.

"I am in favor," she heard now — Countess Dolph was speaking — "of opening the letter in order to see whether it really does contain others, as Felicitas believes. If so, we will distribute them; if not, we will send back to our friend his 'twelve pages, closely and elegantly written, a little manuscript' unread, because we are so terribly discreet. Agreed, Hermann?"

"No," was the answer. "I will not open a letter that is not addressed to me." He took it, handed it to Count Wolfsberg, and said to him quietly, "Take it, do as you like with it, but let's have no more discussion about it. Everything that reminds Maria of Wolfi upsets her terribly. It's oppressively hot here in the tent," he added, turning to his wife. "Come out into the open, Maria."

He took her arm, which she yielded to him passively, and led her away.

After dinner, Countess Dolph read Tessin's letter aloud to the group in an expert manner. There was a little of everything in it: seriousness and wit, vivid descriptions of the land and the people, a powerful and moving expression of the homesickness that tormented him.

Fée withdrew to her rooms as soon as the reading was over. Shortly thereafter, Countess Dolph, accompanied by Hermann and Miss Ninnemann, retired as well.

Count Wolfsberg remained alone with his daughter.

"Hermann is always right," he said, after a long pause. "I, too, was reluctant to open the letter to the unfortunate Forster. I sent it back to Tessin."

"Thank you, Father," Maria replied, hesitantly and with difficulty. "I might have wished, however, that Count Tessin had been asked to make no further attempts to give me news of himself."

"It shall be done."

They had avoided looking at one another; now suddenly their eyes met. Great tenderness, great sympathy was expressed in his. He extended his hand to her; he wanted to talk.

Maria's mouth twisted with pain, and she made a pleading, defensive gesture.

*　　*　　*

Count Wolfsberg could never endure a long stay at Dornach. The good works to which his daughter wholeheartedly devoted herself went against the grain with him. He found it too unpleasant, he said, to think about the disillusionment she would experience, not now, not in the next few years, but in five, or in ten, and not because of the ingratitude, which was inevitable — after all, she did not expect thanks — but because of the realization that her endeavor to reduce the material and moral destitution of the people had been futile and in some cases harmful. Every endeavor whose outcome is negative is unreasonable and demoralizing.

"These people" — when he said these words, he clenched his teeth, and hatred and cruelty flashed from his eyes — "are lazy, treacherous, incorrigible. Everyone who has believed that they could be influenced to the good has failed. In the beginning, I certainly did not put my hands in my pockets and watch without helping as one idiot after another went to ruin . . . . They cured me of my Christian compassion, they themselves!"

"Do you know, Father, why they succeeded in that? May I tell you?" Maria asked.

"Go on."

"Because you do not love them and they sense it."

"That is fortunate for me and for them. I am thereby spared the fate of a Girondist,[16] and they are spared a new opportunity to show how they repay love. Let it be," he forestalled the objection she wanted to raise. "We two will never convince one another on this issue."

The summer was over; Countess Dolph and Felicitas had also left Dornach. Time passed quietly and uneventfully. Maria, often unwell, did not allow any special consideration of her health. She knew that only one thing could benefit her: to forget herself, to strengthen her power of endurance, by easing the suffering of others. She called those who sought her help "my benefactors." Vice, injustice, and folly found a stubborn opponent in her. Her inexhaustible patience never lacked opportunities to exercise itself. And she was not only invited to help carry the burdens of onerous hardship. There was also very light baggage among that weight, and silly encumbrances that had been taken on arbitrarily.

Lisette was struggling with a burden of that sort and made excessive demands on the sympathy of "her child." She had taken it into her head that what prevented Dr. Weise from asking for her hand was the fear of rejection.

"He lives in such seclusion and can't get along by himself," she confided in her mistress. "No one looks after him. His cuffs are always crumpled and the collar of his shirt was buttoned on backwards the other day."

In addition to her longing for the right to take care of Weise's cuffs and collars, she felt the even greater one to be called "Mrs. Weise, the wife of the doctor." She was so sick of that everlasting "Miss Lisette," "Miss" this and "Miss" that, that she could not bear to hear it any longer. "You speak to him. You tell him I'd say yes," was the usual conclusion to her flood of confidences, and each time she received the answer that her wish could not be granted.

So finally Lisette had no choice but to take matters into her own hands and to intervene in the doctor's and her own destiny. One morning she asked him to take her along in his carriage, which he now drove daily to see a patient in the nearby town; she had some Christmas shopping to do there.

Weise readily agreed. "I'm flattered," he said, as Lisette, in a fur coat and hood, took her seat next to him. "Where may I drop you?" He smiled as he said it, though not with pleasure at her outward appearance, but rather because it occurred to him that he had never before seen a person with a face so like that of the puppets one sees at the fair.

Lisette smiled too. "Are you already thinking of leaving me somewhere? That's not very nice of you." Her upper lip pulled up, revealing little mouse teeth that were very well cared for, but rather worn down. Her allusions gradually became very clear, and she all but hit him over the head with her hints.

The doctor became aware, as he confessed to himself, of certain apprehensions and moved as far away from her as possible.

She viewed that as his hospitable invitation to make herself as comfortable as possible with him, leaned back, and examined his profile. The edge of the long visor of his cap and the point of his nose formed a vertical line. His mouth and chin, on the other hand, retreated abruptly, as though out of respect for the remarkable projection above them. That confounded timidity, which Lisette was resolved to dispatch today, found its expression there.

After a few introductory remarks she thought she would venture to make her play. She did it (the doctor attested to this once he had recovered from the assault) with extreme restraint by asking him if he had ever thought of changing his situation.

"Oh, yes, certainly, years ago," he sighed and unintentionally pulled up on the reins of the piebald horse, which, gentle as a lamb, halted immediately, but started off again at the cry, "*Allons, allons!*"[17]

"And never again? That's a shame, and it's also sad." She winked at him mischievously, which made him indignant and anxious. He felt so helpless and so utterly in her power in that infinite solitude. As far as the eye could see, there was nothing but snow and more snow and not a single living thing but the horse, a few crows, and the woman who was making "advances" to him.

She spoke a great deal, and everything she said was either flattering to him or to her, and so he could do nothing but murmur either "Miss Lisette is too kind" or "Miss Lisette is right."

"Such a man," she said now, indulgently, "and he has no hearth."

"Pardon me, but I have, I have — an excellent one, the newest model."

"A domestic one, I mean. Such a man — and he has no wife."

"Excuse me — I have that too."

Miss Lisette turned sideways so quickly that one might have called it *tossing* herself to one side. "You — you have — a wife?"

"Yes, of course, a very pretty one."

"Where?"

"With her parents. I gave her to her parents to keep."

"That is to say," corrected Lisette, who had suddenly lost all sense of tact, "you threw her out?"

"Please, please! One does not take such indelicate action against a lady whom one has already made unhappy by imbuing her with something quite noxious."

His listener was horribly alarmed; she thought of poison.

He whispered, however, "Antipatheia."

"Heavens! What is that?" Lisette cried.

"An incurable and therefore quite pernicious malady, because it robs humans of their loveliest illusion, that of free will. Imagine a woman who is animated by the best intentions toward her husband, a woman who, at just the moment when she should put those into practice, is seized by the fiercest temptation — to throw something at his head . . . and is only rarely able to resist it. And yet not at all incapable of tender emotions — oh, no! Although it was not ordained that the object of those emotions would be able to arouse them except — at a distance. The further he was from her, the more devoted a wife she became. So one day he said to her, paraphrasing a poet, 'It would be well, Carissima, if, in order to love me more, you were to remove yourself from me forever.' She did so, and since then we have had the most exemplary marriage. Recently we celebrated our silver anniversary by mail."

Miss Lisette wanted to express a rather derisive pity for this "type of relationship" — but the doctor said, "In any case, there is one good thing about it: a man who already possesses a wife cannot be expected to take another one."

Lisette opened her eyes wide and looked terribly foolish; she did not say another word. She was so devastated that she made all of her purchases in town without haggling over them. Three weeks passed before she had recovered from her disappointment. Then "her child" again became her primary interest and the adored victim of her affectionate petty tyranny.

As at the close of the previous year, Countess Agathe arrived at Dornach at the close of this one. She helped to decorate the Christmas trees for young and old, for rich and poor, in the hall and in the drawing room. But she alone presided over the lighting of the candles.

Maria was not able to witness the happiness whose preparation had been her principal task for weeks and weeks. On Christmas Eve she gave birth to a second son. He was as delicate and small as the first had been big and strong. With anxious, unexpressed concern, Hermann looked at Countess Agathe as he went with her to the cradle of the newborn.

"No," she said, "he is not weak, just delicate. He will live — a joy to me. Of your children, this one will be mine." Gentler than one had ever seen her, she lost herself in contemplation of the little boy and held her hand over him as though blessing him. "He has dark eyes, Hermann, your father's eyes, and shall be called Erich, like your father."

Maria was in poor health for a long time and could not nurse this child; she did not have as much love for him as for the older one. She did not ask for him, did not resist when he was carried out of her room, and yet he caused no one any difficulty and made very few demands of those around him. He would often lie completely still with his eyes wide open.

"He has a stranger's eyes and his mother's face," decided the nurse, whenever someone tried to determine whom the child resembled. A trace of the anguish of mind that had accompanied his development was reflected in his tiny countenance, and with mournful surprise he seemed to ask, "So this is what your world looks like?"

He suffered no lack of love. Hermann melted before him with overflowing compassion; all the women in the house were devoted to the child, who had something "so unique" about him; his brother defended him like a little lion against the outbursts of their tenderness and then immediately put him in danger of being smothered by the vehemence of his own.

The winter passed; Maria remained weary and exhausted. All the doctors who were consulted recommended, as Dr. Weise had done long ago, a stay of several months in Italy.

The invalid resisted leaving home, but for the first time Hermann decisively opposed his wife's wishes, and she was forced to yield.

Countess Agathe came to Dornach to care for the children in their parents' absence; Hermann and Maria began their journey. Years ago, with her father, she had visited the land that inspires longing in everyone of artistic feeling. She now rediscovered the sentiments of her girlhood in the enjoyment of the wonders of a fairy-tale abundance of nature and of a world where "mortals have created the immortal." How often she breathed freely and easily and saw her own image as pure as it was reflected in the soul of her husband. Her faltering health was strengthened; her shaken courage was fortified.

It was morbid, she thought, to believe that a moment's error could not be atoned for by an entire lifetime of rectitude and performance of duty. Away with the ghosts of a past she had renounced. They were the enemies of happiness — Hermann's happiness. Preserving that was her most important task, compared to which everything else was insignificant. The sight of his joy filled her with her own. Her gaiety, however, warmed his soul; he lived from her life.

"We are on our honeymoon," he would say. His wife, the mother of his children, often seemed to him now like a bride-to-be, but not like the reserved, proud one she had been — no, like a loving one.

And then he would kneel before her and adore her.

Once he exclaimed, "I am too happy; I don't deserve it. I have a debt to pay, but instead of demanding its due, fate overwhelms me again and again with gifts of grace."

"You have a debt to pay?" asked Maria.

"The most grievous one possible — I must pay for a transgression against you. I asked for your hand, I obtained your consent by begging, although I knew you did not give it gladly. The first kiss, beloved, was pressed on your lips by someone you did not love. It was a crime against you — one beyond atonement."

She started at the words.

He took her hands in his. "Maria, *when* will I, *how* will I be punished for that?"

"Never, not at all," she stammered, disconcerted, and pressed her face against his chest.

* * *

They returned home. It was evening when they arrived. The children were asleep. Hermann puffed up his cheeks; his little fists were tightly clenched. He had grown tall and strong, a little boy like a vigorous sapling. Erich, the small, spurious offshoot grafted onto the genuine Dornach family tree, slumbered lightly, started, and opened his eyes as his mother drew near. She was dismayed and discomfited by the mysterious charm that surrounded this child, turned away quickly, and went to the open window.

Fragrant scents filled the air; the trees rustled melodiously; diaphanous mists veiled the meadows; a light haze lay on the heights.

From the road that led to the village, far away, one heard the singing of the women who worked in the fields as they returned home. Nearer and nearer came the sounds of a melancholy Slavic folk song. One could already distinguish the last words of the song:

> Beauty, your splendor,
> Love, your delight,
> All has departed,
> All taken flight.
> Ever true,
> Always new,
> Day by day,
> Is remorse, icy gray.

XIII.

Near Dornach, two young couples had recently taken up residence on the long uninhabited estate of Rakonic. The husbands were brothers; the wives were sisters. They belonged to the highest social circles and, with innate and energetically developed talent, devoted themselves to sport as though it were their profession. Moreover, there were no better judges in cases of rather intricate questions of honor than Counts Clemens and Gustav and no models more worthy of imitation on points of true elegance than Countesses Carla and Betty Wonsheim. There were also nowhere in the world four people in such complete harmony in their views of life, their circumstances, their good behavior, their childlike ignorance. The familial resemblance of the brothers was immediately apparent. Both were of medium height and broad-shouldered, already slightly balding; by nature they were exceedingly composed; they spoke slowly and in the same deliberate manner. The sisters, on the other hand, were very different in appearance. Carla, the oldest, slender and blond, resembled Schwind's Melusine.[18] Betty, dark and small, tended toward plumpness and, as a result, subjected herself to rather rigorous "training." She prided herself on never having ridden with anything but a two-handed surcingle.[19] "What kind of rapport can one have with the horse," she would ask, "if one is sitting on such a machine of a saddle?" Her vivacity formed a pleasant contrast to the sedate behavior of her relatives. She was very much in love with her Clemens; he approved of her affections and had, although he had been a married a whole year, not yet been unfaithful to his little wife. Gustav and Carla, on the other hand, behaved toward one another more like two good comrades than like a young married couple. Every good marital relationship ends in friendship; they had saved themselves the circuitous route and had begun with the friendship right away.

As soon as the banners on the towers of Castle Dornach announced the presence of the master and mistress of the house, the Wonsheims presented themselves and became frequent and welcome guests. However, they also expected a return of their visits and interest in their pursuits. It annoyed them all when Maria would refuse one of their invitations because she was "busy." And with what? Establishing nurseries, building a home for the poor, an infirmary, "and always acting as though she had to be present — if that isn't affectation," they said, "then we no longer know anything at all about such things."

Once they were accosted by a drunken beggar who, when asked where he was from, had answered, "Dornach."

"What — from Dornach? Are there poor people left in Dornach? Isn't it a paradise for the poor?"

The ne'er-do-well winked slyly and said in a plaintive tone, "For the poor director of the infirmary and the supervisors, and whatever that sweet rabble calls itself — for them it's probably heaven on earth; they take it easy and get fat. The real poor have it as hard in Dornach as they do everywhere else."

That was grist for the mill of the Wonsheims, and they did not take the source into account.

One day, when yet another refusal from Dornach arrived, Betty flung the letter that contained it out the open window, so that it sliced through the air and flew far away. "The fourth rejection from that tiresome creature!" she cried, and Clemens answered, "You're as persistent as bedbugs. Leave her alone."

"Absolutely not! We cannot allow her to sit and mope in her infirmary. We have to stir her up a little."

Betty's opinion prevailed.

"Let's stir, then," Gustav and Carla replied, and the very next morning, quite early, the family arrived at full gallop at Dornach to invite Hermann and Maria to go riding.

They were a charming sight as they waited in the courtyard, the distinguished-looking men and the graceful women on their fine steeds, whose every sinew was powerful and whose every drop of blood, pure. They were accompanied by Flick and Flock, their grave, intelligent mastiffs, who, regardless of the pace, followed close on the hooves of the horses as though tethered to them. They looked neither to the right nor to the left, they disregarded both a bird taking flight and a startled hare, but a glance, a friendly cry from their masters, was answered with delighted barking and joyous leaps. Right now they were sulking over the interruption of their morning run.

"Confounded waiting! How much longer will this take?" said Flick to Flock.

"Smell, just smell!" replied the other. "The dogs are already coming with their humans. That Boxl, I'd like to thrash him till he doesn't know which way is up." He growled; his coat bristled.

Boxl ran up to him, small and impudent; his whole body was an insolent question: "What do you think you're doing here?"

"I'm here to leave my toothprints in your hide, you rat," and Flock wanted to leap upon him. But his master commanded, "Lie down!" So he closed his eyes halfway, licked his muzzle, and turned his back on the quarrelsome Boxl, who never stopped barking unpleasant things at him.

Flick sat down close to him, and the two of them stretched their necks, wagged their tails, opened their massive jaws, and yawned loudly and challengingly.

In the meantime, the Wonsheims' invitation had been accepted. Maria went to change into her riding clothes, and the horses were brought out: Hermann's brown gelding and Maria's darling, Hadassa, sadly neglected of late.

Five years old, with a fine head, slender neck, broad chest and back, she danced along on buoyant, flawless feet. She looked like cloudy grey marble, and her thin mane and her tail, which tapered off at the end, were raven black. When she saw the strange horses, she threw up her head; her dark brown eyes, which protruded from her lean face, flashed. She puffed out her nostrils, neighed threateningly, and rose suddenly on her hind legs, so that the little groom who was holding fast to the bridle dangled in the air like a handkerchief.

Everyone laughed. Maria stepped up to the mare and stroked her neck. Hadassa, however, chewing the bit and pawing the sand, pulled back sullenly from her mistress.

"Nervous?" asked the latter and sprang into the saddle with Hermann's help.

She had not intended to begin the day with amusement; she had had a great deal planned for today and was at first displeased by the interruption. Soon, however, she felt that it had been a good deed. The rapid motion in the dewy coolness of the morning had a refreshing and invigorating effect on her. The mist dissolved; the sun rose behind the leafy forests, which the autumn had already richly colored, and eclipsed their painted moribundity.

The riders chose a path through the park. They came by the vantage point where Maria's first conversation with her brother had taken place, where she had exchanged the first words with the one who had paved the way for her crime.

"Past — past . . . carry me away, Hadassa!" and without thinking she struck the shoulder of the skittish animal with her whip. Hadassa's indignation knew no bounds. She reared, kicked, and set an example of obstinate insubordination that the other horses began to follow.

"Nothing can be done with her. I must get her by herself," said Maria. "We'll meet at the hunting lodge." And declining every offer of company, even Hermann's, she left the path for the newly plowed field nearby, in whose soft, deep soil Hadassa would run till she was weary. A green and grassy hollow bordered on the field and formed the bank of the clear, full stream. It was the same one that, up in the mountains, at the foot of the castle ruins, raged with such magnificent bravado through the rocks.

Even from afar Maria could see its smooth surface glisten. There, taking its placid course in the shallow river bed, it had lost its rage.

"You see, Hadassa, even for a fury completely different from yours, the rise and fall of high tide is followed by the calm ebb of equilibrium. You don't believe you'll be tamed, you wild one? Just wait till you're tired." Leaning forward almost onto the mare's neck, she gave the horse her head. A mad and joyous ride, a flight over ditches and hedges. Hadassa no longer feels the earth beneath her feet. Hadassa is an eagle, is the storm; to be carried by her and to feel so much life, strength, and fire subject to your caprice, to the pressure of your hand — that is happiness. Let those who do not know this happiness deny it . . . . Maria's heart opened itself to it with rapture. She breathed freely and refreshed; once again she was blissful and calm, and within her there was peace . . . .

Where had she sought this peace? In the performance of duty, in charity, in the art she practiced with enthusiasm. To no avail. Inner peace was to be found on Hadassa's back, in the wild delight of a meaningless race. The frothing steed, the glowing rider are seized by the same frenzy. Hadassa cannot be wearied, only inflamed, and Maria is no longer so sure of her mastery over her. All the more glorious — long live danger! Face to face with danger, it is easier to forget . . . .

Now she had thought it, and the spell was broken. To think of forgetting of course means to remember. A scream rose from Maria's breast and resounded weirdly through the silence. But listen — there was an answer: a dull, monotonous sound that came from a distance. At the entrance to the forest glen was a mill, and its gigantic wheel turned ceaselessly, driven by the falling stream . . . .

Onward, toward it! Hadassa does not swerve. A bitter smile twisted Maria's mouth. Life is poor, even in invention. Everything repeats itself. This is just what had happened years ago when she, hardly more than a child, was carried toward the death she now races to meet. A hideous death between the black and dripping spokes of the wheel — at that time she had dreaded it, but today she dreads only hideous existence . . . .

Pale, her eyes wide open, she approached her goal with frightening speed.

Then she experienced something strange. Is it always like that before the end? Infinite light illuminates the depths of the soul; the roots of emotions and actions are unveiled. Stripped of their deceptive shimmer, the illusions of the senses and the imagination show themselves to be loathsome distortions. But pure feeling, previously repressed by the illusions, shines forth in magnificent splendor. Now two motherless children travel the familiar paths. Now the heart of the best of all men is desolate . . . . Why? Why? It should not have been like that — what a shame that this happiness has been destroyed!

"Maria!" a voice rose above the rushing of the stream, "Maria!" and she, called back suddenly into the awareness of reality, started and pulled up on the reins.

Hadassa reared and then stood with her feet wide apart, with her nostrils steaming and her ears laid back. Where had her mad run taken her? What sort of a water-spewing monster was this, into whose jaws she had been about to leap?

She was frightened, and at the same time pleased, because from the same corner where the roaring horror was up to its mischief, her good companion and stable neighbor, brown Bob, came trotting up.

He, too, was agitated, but his rider was quite composed and called, "What happened? Did she get out of control?"

Maria stammered an indistinct "No." She felt like a criminal overtaken in flight. In the midst of an almost superhuman struggle for self-control, she began to tremble; a shiver ran through her. The eyes of the one to whom she had de-voted her last thoughts rested on her face. Did it reflect the battles she had just fought?

Hermann turned his horse and now rode beside her past the mill. He leaned toward Maria, laid his hand on hers, and said, "You're very pale."

"Really?" She pulled out her handkerchief and pressed it to her brow.

"I was worried that Hadassa — she's having a bad day — might not want to pass the mill alone. So I brought an escort."

"But how did you get here?"

"Across the field. You went around it; I headed you off."

"And you still had the time to trot up in stately deliberation to meet me? That's also a feat. Bravo, Bob!" She patted the neck of the horse, who was cov-ered with sweat and froth. "I love you."

Hermann smiled broadly at her. "He's lucky; his master envies him."

"He has no reason to," she said earnestly and tenderly.

He pressed her hand, which he still held in his own. "You say that as though you were sorry about it," he responded in his earlier tone. His gaze expressed sheer happiness and awakened a reflection in Maria's soul.

What had dawned on her before now pervaded her with the light and with the strength of a conviction as clear as sunshine. What was best and highest in her, that in which all the noble qualities of her soul culminated, was the love that had matured slowly, her love for this man.

XIV.

From then on Maria did not require much urging to join in when the Wonsheims were "up to something." She soon exchanged the role of a spectator for that of a participant and finally for that of a leader. She wanted noble sport to be undertaken in the lofty manner of an art, rather than with the sobriety of a trade. The hunt, for instance, which Carla and Betty pursued passionately. What was practiced with such skill should also be practiced with elegance.

"Let's do something nice for them," she said to Hermann. "Let's revive the golden age of the hunt for a few days; we'll conjure up the court of August the Strong[20] or the hunting castle of Blankenburg. Let's give a party that will show what the House of Dornach can do. Just think — I myself have never seen it in all its splendor."

"A grievous omission," he responded, "but we will make amends for it."

The deserted, draped and covered staterooms were opened to light and air, and something like an awakening coursed through the rooms. A faint rustle arose in the old carving and paneling of the walls, a rippling sound in the sea-green, gold-fringed curtains and draperies, puffed up by the wind that surged in through the windows. The prisms of the crystal chandeliers knocked merrily against one another with a clear, delicate sound. And in the orchestra pit of the ballroom, what doings there! There was tuning and practicing and the rehearsing of Strauss. It was a tempestuous resurrection for the stringed- and the wind-instruments, which had been resting in their caskets since they had lent their voices to the long-forgotten melody of a minuet *à la reine*.[21] The aged, dour caretaker of the castle, who viewed himself as its real master, reached grudgingly enough for his keys at Hermann's urging. And the ironbound oak cupboards in the silver chamber yielded up the treasures that their guardian polished so carefully and hid so jealously from the inquisitive eyes of the laity. Now they emerged and ornamented the tables in the large banquet hall, the fanciful centerpieces and drinking horns, the nautilus shells, the Roman goblets and the Gothic ones, with their tiny filigreed towers, pointed arches, and spires. Tankards, cups, and bowls of admirable embossed work, with figures in relief, covered with enamel, or inlaid with precious stones: triumphs of the goldsmith's art, betraying the hand of Jamnitzer, Eisenhoidt, and Dinglinger,[22] those modest masters of art in miniature, from whose workshops so many great artists have emerged.

The invitations to the party were composed in the style of the eighteenth century. The "cavaliers and dames" were requested to appear for dinner, after the battue that would take the place of the historic fox hunt, "dressed in green velvet laced with silver." For the hunt itself the guests would of course dress as they pleased.

"The shabbier, the chic-ier!" Carla and Betty Wonsheim, who had invented the word, took it seriously; still, they did not look their best in their crumpled hats, their old overcoats, short skirts, and worn-out laced boots.

But if the gentlemen have their leather hunting-breeches used to scrub floors in order to eradicate every semblance of newness, the ladies can do no less, and their outfits must also bear the traces of a hundred bloody battles against furred and feathered game.

When the guests were assembled, the procession took place, which was loosely based on Döbel[23] and led by Willi, Wilhelm's oldest son, his unsheathed hunting knife in hand. It was a delightful spectacle, lacking neither the crowd in the garb of the legendary forest dwellers nor the virtuoso who could play the bagpipes nor the huntsman who knew how to blow the hunting-horn melodiously.

The company applauded at length and, in high spirits, climbed into the wagons that would bring them to the grounds where the first battue was to take place. The last one would bring the hunters back toward the manor house in the afternoon, and Maria, yielding to the entreaties of the others, promised to participate in it.

At the appointed hour she left the house. It was cold; a sharp north wind had arisen. It swept the thin, hard snow into the ditches and gullies and from time to time blew a shower of delicate icy needles over the fields.

Quietly and without speaking, the hunters approached; those who directed each flank were in front. The marshall called a halt. Now the procession split up and, between two beaters, each hunter moved into position.

Maria had not taken part in a battue since her childhood, and she had retained only a muddled impression of it. Now she walked with Clemens, whom she had earlier that morning promised to accompany and who now seemed quite peculiar to her. His face, usually so impassive, revealed intense excitement, but he remained silent.

The circle closed and the hunters began to advance.

Everything was still motionless in the shallow field, lightly covered with snow, which sloped down evenly and then rose up again toward the fence that enclosed the park.

"The hares were clever," Maria said. "They've all gone off to the forest."

"They're here; they're just hiding," answered Clemens.

The beaters began to shake their rattles. A ragged boy in socks full of holes jumped about in front of Maria, obviously wanting to attract her attention. He really did raise a hare. Then three others followed, four, six . . . . The first shot rang out, and a large, fat hare fell and lay motionless.

"That was Betty," Clemens murmured, and an expression of fervent envy quivered around his mouth. His hands trembled; he shot and missed, shot again and hit the mark, but badly. His victim jumped on three legs into the next hunter's shot. Now he pulled himself together; now he was himself again. Happy the hare that came within his range: it did not suffer long.

The circle grew smaller and smaller; the ground teemed with game. It seemed to grow out of the earth, rose up from every furrow, leapt from behind every clod of dirt, used all its tricks in vain, rushed about in the madness of fear, shrieked so that it might have moved a stone to pity — and entertained the hunters. And particularly the common folk! What a holiday the common folk had!

To drive the most timid, most completely defenseless animals together to a spot where they can be merrily shot down, and then to lend a helping hand in clubbing them to death when the rifle has only half accomplished its work, to do that to one's heart's content and even to get money for it — that is a treat for the poor man and a useful lesson for his child.

The last beat, the best beat. Who would have thought it! Most of the gentlemen and all of the ladies were seized by frenzy. Faced with such quantities of game, even the most cold-blooded hunter is set on fire. The ABCs of his science are forgotten. He hardly aims; he does not care whether "the target" is shot to bits.

The ground is covered with dead, dying, mutilated animals. They enrich the soil with their blood; their necks are broken and twisted by the beaters, who tie the hind legs together and load their sticks with the still twitching booty.

Maria had turned away. She was filled with revulsion, disgust, and a profound amazement — these people who are delighting in the agony of a wretched creature, these are all good people.

"Countess, look here," cried Clemens with his cheeriest laugh.

An old, blind hare had placed itself about ten feet away from him and was sitting up on its hind legs. Both ears had been shot off, and the blood ran down over his sightless eyes. He slowly wiped it away with his front paws, shook himself, bent his round head to the right and to the left, then lowered it sadly and looked unbelievably foolish.

"I beg you, put him out of his misery," said Maria.

Clemens fired. The hare fell — and not far from him the little beater as well, who shrieked at the top of his lungs and stretched one leg in the air.

"Bungler!" Betty called over.

At the same moment, the horn gave the signal that the hunt was over.

Maria had rushed to the wounded boy; Clemens followed her slowly. Dr. Weise came with giant strides. He wore a cap with ear flaps, was wrapped in a fur coat that made him resemble a sentry-box, and was laden with twice as much hunting equipment as he could have used. With difficulty he knelt down beside the boy, examined him thoroughly, and said, "My diagnosis is that the *sura* of the left leg of this *adolescentulus* has been grazed by buckshot."

"Is that all it is, really?"

Weise nodded. "That is all."

Now the youth let out a scream that made his earlier ones seem like mere sighs. He raved and shrieked, "I got one. The doctor doesn't want me to have it; the doctor is lying. I got one, I got hit, and I get five guilders!"

"Always the same old act," said Clemens.

The doctor replied, however, after he had boxed the patient's ears and stood up with the help of two hunters, "Pardon me, but that is your fault, Count. When one pays every beater who's been shot five guilders for the pellets in him, then one must not be surprised that the people want to take this easy opportunity to earn something."

*　*　*

In three rooms of the castle the guests were wined and dined "*magnifique.*" Hermann stood up and emptied his glass "to the health of the worthy hunters." The horns were blown, and for the finale the huntsman's apprentices sounded the hunting cry.

It was the most stylish banquet imaginable and was executed with far more historical accuracy than most of the group was able to appreciate. Still, all were pleased by the rich display, by the variety and the elegance of the costumes.

Carla Wonsheim particularly aroused admiration; she looked enchanting in her green velvet gown, trimmed with white satin, and in the dark plumed hat on her pretty head. It seemed as though she had stood in a shower of diamonds: she was sprinkled from head to toe with these sparkling gems.

"Who are you supposed to be, Countess?" asked Baroness Wlasta Wynohrad, a slender young woman of the landed gentry, with strikingly pretty eyes. The Wonsheim ladies had risen like stars on her limited horizon, and she knew no greater ambition than to be admitted to the company of her idols.

"Who am I supposed to be? The mistress of the house can tell you that," Carla answered. "It was she who dictated our costumes."

"Not mine! *I* never allow myself to be dictated to. In my circle people dance to my tune. Eighteenth century, hunting dress — *va bene.*[24] Everything else is up to me."

Carla ran her eyes distantly over the baroness's evening dress and thought, "None too presentable, the good woman."

The latter drew up her thin shoulders, stretched her long neck, and imparted the glad tidings that she would be spending the next winter in Vienna.

"Oh?" said Carla.

"Oh, yes, and I'll be coming to you often to ask you to take me under your wing. Viennese society is so unfriendly to newcomers."

"Only when they are not *comme-il-faut*."[25]

"Oh, but of course — I feel the same way myself . . . . Oh, heavens, look! The Wilhelms are already starting to dance. Come, Carla — oh, dear!" she interrupted herself. "I've said the wrong thing; please forgive me!"

Her apology was acknowledged with a mere nod. She was still not deterred. "Let's go into the other room," she said and took the countess's arm familiarly.

"My, my!" Carla laughed, "the two of us seem to be on very intimate terms! I was not aware of that."

Wlasta blushed deeply, and Carla continued mercilessly, "And why not, as neighbors here in the country? That does not necessarily mean anything — in the city, I mean. There one is always so busy. You see, dear Baroness, I couldn't name a single hour when you might find me available."

The baroness was close to being physically overcome with mortification. She struggled to catch her breath and, with downcast eyes and faltering voice, uttered the words, "My maiden name is Zastrisl."

"You don't say!" Carla responded with cheerful amazement to this dazzling revelation. Then, followed by her now very melancholy shadow, she moved toward Maria, who was sitting on a sofa facing the open door of the ballroom, surrounded by several extremely attentive gentlemen.

"The baroness," she said, "would like to know who I'm supposed to be."

"You are," came the answer, "the living reproduction of a portrait of the wife of Duke Rudolf of Brunswick-Lüneburg."

"Lüneburg? Never heard of it."

"Nor I, but I'll make a note of it," said Betty, who had also approached and who now laid a hand on Maria's shoulder. "One learns so much at Dornach. Everything possible is done to educate the guests. I'll bet you arranged the party today only in order to teach us something about history and geography behind our backs."

"One can certainly approve of lessons like that," Carla interjected, and Betty cried, "Oh, how I enjoyed myself! It was so much fun."

"And what did you enjoy most?" asked Maria.

"The hunt, of course. I shot thirty-one hares and a fox, although my envious husband disputes the latter. And you've enjoyed yourself too, haven't you?"

"Not during the hunt."

The little woman was utterly amazed. "How can that be?"

"It struck me that we were taking pleasure in agony. The sight of those piteously maltreated creatures upset me."

"Excuse me, Countess, but that is sentimentality," said a youthful, somewhat affected diplomat.

"Says thoughtlessness itself," Maria responded in an undertone, as though speaking to herself.

He, however, seethed with indignation; he almost leapt to his feet. Just yesterday a few of the friends who were present tonight had been speaking of Maria's unapproachability, and he, swaggering, had said with obvious intent, "Yes, indeed, it is not easy to please her. One must be witty."

And now — and, moreover, in the presence of the witnesses to his boasting — "Thoughtlessness!" He wanted to make a cutting reply, but since nothing particularly appropriate occurred to him, he decided to remain silent. He was consoled for the little humiliation he had suffered, however, when Carla turned to him with the words, "I still owe you a waltz from Carnival.[26] Shall I pay my debt now?"

He rose, very flattered, and whirled away with her.

Cousin Wilhelm, however, who was a great favorite of the Wonsheims, had to dance with Betty in order to do penance for having imprudently expressed the suspicion that she might be tired.

"What? Tired? Me? I'll have a horse brought round at six o'clock tomorrow morning, and I'll ride for a couple of hours."

Wilhelm laughed. "Just the way I was when I was a lieutenant with the Kaiser Nikolaus hussars."

Maria sat musing; her eyes grew more and more fixed as she gazed into the throng of gay and elegantly attired people, and what she saw was strange. The glittering scene of gold-braided gentlemen, of ladies sparkling with jewels, and of old-world magnificence in the room where they moved about became transparent and disappeared, phantom-like, before a deep, dark background. There was a roaring and rumbling like the threatening sounds of a storm-tossed sea. The waves towered to the sky, plunged to unfathomable depths, climbed up only to sink again: an eternal rising and falling.

And a howl of pain burst forth from this ghastly churning of waves — hunted, hunting, devouring, devoured — for they consisted of the bodies of animals and humans, they were the tortured family of the living, and the ocean that drove this tide was an ocean of suffering.

Occasionally a twinkling star appeared high on the horizon, and millions of human hearts rose up, yearning eyes drank in its trembling light. But it was not long till they knew that the glow that smoldered and promised was only the reflection of the longing for comfort, of the hope — in their own hearts.

And onward roll the moaning waves of the ocean of suffering.

But look! What is swimming toward them? A merry band of cheerful men and women in a small vessel bedecked with streamers. They jest, they play, they flirt and float on without a care — toward the same fate that awaits the tormented ones . . . .

"What are you thinking about?" a soft voice asked suddenly. Maria started, as though waking from a dream. Helmi stood beside her.

And others came, and the diplomat paid court to her as though it were a matter of life and death, and Clemens Wonsheim felt, with some discomfort, that he was once again on the verge of falling in love with the wife of one of his acquaintances, and said to himself, "Nonsense — absolutely nothing would come of that."

Once in the course of the evening Maria went to the glass wall of the balcony and pushed back the curtain. There before her lay the broad and snow-covered countryside, shimmering white, clearer than the sky. Oh, this beautiful earthly world, so worthy of adoration and yet filled with pain . . . . Your work, You incomprehensible, unknown God . . . . She remembered a verse she had read in an old book:

> Though to His Providence thou ne'er wouldst bow,
> The beauty of His works thou must avow.

Long ago these words had wounded her religious sentiments . . . long ago!

XV.

The party at Dornach inspired a series of more or less successful imitations. There were balls at all the manor houses in the surrounding area; there was even a dance at the Wilhelms for the first time since they had set up housekeeping. Later the winter sports began, and all participated zealously. Gustav Wonsheim emerged then in all his glory.

"When it freezes," Carla said, "my husband's all aflame."

He went up and down the hills on snowshoes like a Norwegian; he could handle an ice pick like a Dutchman; on the ice rink he put the American champion Haynes[27] to shame. His indefatigability in arranging one new winter pleasure after another was amazing.

In December of that year he, without taking any notice of the fact, won the hearts of sixteen ladies in the neighborhood; however, almost all of them turned from him in February when Hermann won an illustrious victory over him in a reckless sleigh race.

Time flew by. The departure from Dornach and Rakonic for Vienna was put off from one week to the next and finally given up altogether. The spring hunts had begun, and the ladies and gentlemen continued to enjoy themselves splendidly in the country.

Maria led a peculiar double life. One day she was a second Elizabeth of Thuringia,[28] and the next she was a full-blooded sportswoman who often surpassed the stronger sex in daring and "pluck."

"Splendid woman, Dornach's wife," said Clemens to his brother with a sigh.

And Gustav responded between two puffs of his cigarette, "That's true, by God!"

Clemens slid down in his armchair, stretched out his legs, and leaned back his head. "The way she drove up here yesterday!" he said. "Betty called to her suddenly. One jerk — and the horses stopped in their tracks."

"I tell you, there's no better 'four-in-hand' driver than she."

"Such an eye, such a hand — and such composure."

"Hermann, that fellow, he's damned lucky to have a wife like that."

The object of their envy, however, considered what inspired the complete approval of the neighbors an uncanny marvel. He tried to understand Maria's new passion for diversion as a reaction to her earlier melancholy. Oscillations of the soul from one extreme to the other, oscillations that are nothing but the preparation for the soul's return to its lovely and salutary equanimity.

One morning Maria came home from a wild ride through the woods, which were still barely passable. Strands of hair, glistening like silk, had escaped from the heavy braids that could not be forced completely under her hat; tiny, unruly ringlets curled down over her sparkling, excited eyes; her slender nostrils quivered; her white teeth shone from between her slightly parted lips. Hurriedly she related that they had a new engagement with the Wonsheims that evening.

A twinge of jealously shot through her husband's heart, for which he reproached himself immediately. "You enjoyed yourself?" he asked.

"Oh, royally!" she answered; he stroked her flushed cheeks gently and said, "We'll spend the next winter in the city if that suits you. In the country we have too little rest, don't you think?"

"Whatever *you* think," she answered, and his unspoken reproof had its effect.

Maria came to herself. One word from Hermann had awakened her from the frenzy where she had found a kind of peace.

Now she wanted more than its semblance; she wanted to regain true peace itself, without which life is futile and absurd.

She began to seek it in the Book of Books, in the words of the Scripture, which are not addressed to chilly virtue, but to the remorseful sinner. These promises are meant for him; the Father's arms are open to the wretched publican, to the penitent Magdalen.

Maria implored and received absolution from the lips of a venerable priest, yet in her own eyes she remained unabsolved.

"How can your forgiveness help me, Father, when I cannot forgive myself?" she asked, and the elderly pastor responded, "Has my daughter forgotten that it is not my forgiveness that she receives in the confessional, but that of the All-merciful?"

"If it is God's forgiveness, why don't I feel its blessings? Why do I leave God's table with as heavy a heart as I approached it?"

In vain her spiritual advisor offered countless consoling arguments from the inexhaustible fount of the faith of which he was a true disciple.

She knelt before him in the confessional of the castle chapel, hid her face in her hands, and sobbed.

The priest looked sorrowfully at the struggling woman and said, after long contemplation, "The ways of the Lord are inscrutable. It sometimes happens that pure men and women succumb to temptation with God's permission. This occurs in order to prevent such people from priding themselves on their godliness. They fell, yes — but at the feet of the All-bountiful, whom they had forgotten in their transgression and to whom their remorse has returned them. They lie there henceforth in humility and contrition, nearer to the heart of the eternal God than a hundred righteous ones."

He gave her his blessing. She rose silently to her feet and never again spoke to him of her pain.

The elderly clergyman, however, bowed his bald head to the ground in devout simplicity before the image of the crucified Savior and said an ardent prayer of thanks, "All glory be to God that You have placed in the mouth of Your unworthy servant the words that have saved a soul from despair."

Maria now traveled her path alone and no longer sought oblivion or support. She had finally achieved outward equanimity. That helped her to conceal her agonies of soul; indeed, her outward serenity increased as she strove for perfection. She was ruthless with herself, even in fulfilling the smallest of duties — and had failed in her first and highest. She carried the most refined sense of justice within her — and beside her, the fruit of injustice grew; an intruder, a little thief, who enjoyed that to which he had no right. Maria's sentiments for the child did not extend beyond a painful sympathy.

But Hermann, both father and son, seemed to want to compensate him for the tenderness his mother denied him. The four-year-old heir, a tall, sturdy boy who carried himself as boldly and as proudly as though the earth belonged to him, melted with love and devotion before the "little one." Combative by nature and always ready to lift his little fists to strike a blow, he displayed amazing patience with his younger brother's every whim. He would rein in his wooden horses in the midst of the wildest gallop if Erich cried, in a tearful voice, "Enough — the horses are tired now."

Smiling benevolently, Hermann would watch as Erich hid the horses from him under a bench in the garden, fed them, and covered them up with his handkerchief.

The bigger one protected the smaller one on any number of occasions; the latter protected the dogs from Hermann's rough affection. On this matter the two would come to blows, but they were always dealt by the weaker boy.

One strong bond between the two siblings was the delight the one had in telling stories and the delight of the other in hearing them. Erich's eyes were almost worshipful as he listened to his brother's stories. These tales bore a remarkable resemblance to one another and always concerned the desert, a storm, and lions. Sometimes, when the desert grew so vast that it was larger than the meadow over there beyond the stream, and when the storm became too wild and the lions too bloodthirsty, a shiver would run through the little one; his tiny face would grow long, he would clench his fingers tightly around his knees, and let his head fall to his chest.

Pleased with the success of his narrative skills, Hermann would throw back his head and cry, "And I will go there and shoot the lions dead!"

This was the height of his triumph, and he enjoyed it undisturbed until one day the little one jumped up, stretched out his arms, and, full of enthusiasm, said, "And Erich will go there first and give the lions something to eat."

From that moment on he began to indulge himself in his thoughts about the journey to the lions with a persistence far beyond his years. Facing the direction Hermann had designated as the one where the lions lived, he could lose himself entirely in his thoughts, smiling peacefully and happily, as though the loveliest images were arising before him.

His mother resisted the little boy's tendency to daydream. She taught him to play; she was angry when she found him idle. But even her anger was a boon and a blessing to him, for then she concerned herself with him. He listened to her, standing as still as a little statue, and looked up at her adoringly with radiant eyes.

Maria could not long endure the child's look of pleading love.

She turned away from him; she asked herself, shuddering, "Does no one but me see the appalling resemblance?" "No one," answered the candor and the ease of her loved ones, of strangers, of everyone who saw the child and burst into admiration of the charming little being.

His particular admirer was the doctor, although he usually paid no attention to healthy children. "Count Erich is, I hear, intended for the priesthood," he said to Lisette, who had sulked for a long time in his presence but had eventually given it up because he had failed to notice. "But I predict that they won't make a canon out of him. That one won't stay in the country — he'll become a traveler for the Lord, a missionary. He's already a lover of both humans and animals, and he also has that irresistible longing to go out into the world."

Those good souls, Helmi and Wilhelm, often said that they would be happy to have a ninth child, if he were just like Erich. "Such poetically lovely children are usually sickly, but this one is as healthy as a cherub and looks like one too."

Countess Agathe had made that comparison first. Because of her favorite grandson, she tore herself away from her monastic solitude earlier than usual. She submitted with pleasure to Hermann's joking reproach that he would never have guessed she could be as weak and as indulgent as she was toward his second son. He reminded her of his grandfather.

The countess had come up with that, and for the members of both Dornach houses it became family dogma, which meant that it was a tenet that could thwart both common sense and the most profound insight.

As it grew nearer to Carnival, Hermann's mother once again reminded him and Maria of their duties to society. Count Wolfsberg, overwhelmed with business and therefore unable to leave Vienna, longed to see his daughter. Countess Dolph wrote, "You are both too young to bury yourselves in the country. Come to Vienna, although there isn't much going on here. People are becoming more and more foolish and their manners worse and worse. Previously I could always tell whether I was speaking with a hack driver or a *comtesse*; now I constantly confuse the two. You'll see for yourselves whether or not there are still young gentlemen; an old woman who is presumed to have some intellect — the arch enemy of that breed — could consider them extinct. I'm contemplating the idea of organizing literary evenings, but — the writers are all atheists — my Ninny is against it. The good Lord and I are at variance over this particular soul. I think I'll let Him have her.

"Your Wonsheims called on me. Both of the men are in love with you, Maria; two raccoons pining for the morning star. As soon as your name is mentioned, their faces snap into an expression of humility.

"Their better halves are beginning to withdraw, for reasons that one — probably in order to disguise the bitter reality — calls 'interesting.'

"Dear child, my Horace Walpole puts his prototype to shame; he writes me letters that are not only admirable and entertaining, but affectionate as well. Naturally he is not risking much at this distance. Such is my fate. The only clever bachelor on earth, and there are oceans between us. Always the same old story; everything is a repetition in this world, which is itself not the good Lord's original creation, but a copy of a model constructed by the devil. I have it from a reliable source.

"And now I say again: come! Pull yourselves away from your bucolic friends Wilhelm and Helmi, to whom I send my regards, and from your peasants, who love your money, your hot soup, and your warm jackets.

"And finally, the news of the day: Alma is in Vienna. We had heard that she was shriveling up with boredom in her castle in the woods. So your father wrote her a compassionate lie: 'Your friends miss you; why are you staying away?' She wrote back, 'I will stay away forever' and — was here."

"Will you see her?" Hermann asked.

Maria blushed to the roots of her hair. "Yes."

"So you can forgive her?"

"Me? What right do I have — or does anyone have," she corrected herself, flustered by his surprise at these words. "Who is so pure, who stands so tall, that he may presume to say, 'I forgive the sins of others.'"

* * *

A few weeks later she encountered Alma at a ball, greeted her first, received her visit the next day, and returned it.

Princess Tessin thanked her with tears in her still beautiful eyes.

Maria's friendship had always been the proud possession she could call on in the struggle between her fear of the world's opinion and her love for Wolfsberg. Two strong sentiments in one weak heart, which was unable to defy the one or give up the other. She had therefore made her way through life, exceedingly polite, exceedingly kind, seeing in everyone who approached her a judge, whom she sought to bribe. When Maria had begun to avoid her, it had seemed to her as though the last veil had been torn from her transparent secret. Now, however, her protector had returned, and she felt herself rehabilitated, as far as it was possible, in the eyes of the world whose judgment took the place of conscience with her.

Count Wolfsberg expressed neither approval nor disapproval of the resumption of contact between his daughter and Alma. They gradually fell back into the old patterns. Wolfsberg was occasionally a little sarcastic about "the good princess"; Maria defended her, although not quite as warmly as before.

Aunt Dolph's perception proved to be correct: both Wonsheims were in love, without any hope of a response, with their neighbor from the country. The latter had "slackened off" considerably of late, but she was and remained — one particularly noticed it in the city, where there were countless opportunities for comparison — more beautiful, elegant, and appealing than anyone else.

The brothers went out into society solely on her account. Betty and Carla, who had recently become mothers, were confined to the house. The Wonsheims dismissed congratulations on their new fatherhood — "Oh, please, they're only girls."

Hermann, that good fellow, got one son after another, and they got — girls. They sought consolation for this deplorable outcome in all sorts of diversions.

One of these was the "fun" they derived from associating with Fée. They were her confidants: she told them everything and more. For instance, that she was carrying on an overseas correspondence and that she now took life very seriously; yes, like a certain someone whom she regarded as her model, she even looked at its darkest side. That she was learning to manage money and frequently paid her bills with her own — naturally, gloved — hands, and that she read the stock report every day. It could happen that one might be obliged to sell some bonds in order to cover the costs of a long journey, which might even be a honeymoon.

Countess Dolph, with whom Fée spent most of her time and who, like the Wonsheim brothers, had also been initiated into all of her secrets, did not reproach her for her talkativeness.

"In the world, which is nothing but an extended family, one knows everything about everyone else anyway," she said to Fée one evening in Maria's presence.

"Do you really believe that?" asked the latter. "I think that the world and its families know almost nothing about their members. I, at least," she burst out suddenly, "prefer the slighted and have an aversion to the adored."

"Then you should find yourself suspect," Dolph replied.

"Perhaps I do," said Maria.

Aunt Dolph shrugged her shoulders in apparent unconcern; inwardly, however, a quiet, recurring, uncomfortable suspicion arose. "Did Tessin's love perhaps not go unrewarded? . . . Pah! Those who cannot resist the irresistible are excused," she added mentally and said, "Forgive me, but that is morbid exaggeration."

Only rarely did Maria give way to expressions of that sort. They were extorted from her by the fear in her heart, by desperate temptation: "Anticipate the disclosure yourself — it can happen at any time — by chance, which is the mysterious ruler of the world and which no power on earth can avert."

These were difficult moments, but Maria also had periods of inner peace: those when she succeeded in forgetting. With prudent deliberation, with endless exertion, she practiced acquiring this great art, which has freed many a soul.

She lived through the present, through the alleviation of the suffering she encountered, through her shy love for her husband, through the care she gave with joy and anguish to her children. Often she repeated her consoling maxim to herself: "An entire lifetime of rectitude can compensate for an hour of error . . . . Can it?" — the tormenting doubt within her raised its voice — "Perhaps, if this life were not so sweet, if the consequences of the error did not live and breathe."

XVI.

Over the course of the winter Countess Agathe had often expressed the desire to have her children and grandchildren visit her as soon as they left the city. They came, and the countess requested again and again that they postpone their departure. Because of Erich — the child had captivated her. Hermann often followed her with his eyes as she walked stiffly and solemnly, looking much older than she was, holding the hand of the little boy she had taken into her heart and on whose account she bitterly regretted that she did not have a way with children.

The child was ill at ease in the presence of this mute love. What was the point of walks that never went anywhere, and when no one even told a story? Erich would make feeble attempts to free his hand from his grandmother's, but then she would say, "Don't you like being with me, Erich?"

Out of fear he suppressed the "No" that was on the tip of his tongue and after a while would ask, disconcerted, "And what will we play now?" whereupon the old lady, after a few awkward attempts to turn his attention to a bird flying past or to a flower by the wayside, would lead him back to the nurse.

It was already summer when the family finally arrived at Dornach. The first mowing of hay was drying in the meadows. The fragrance of the blossoming lime-trees was almost overpowering; the crops stood tall; the birds were in their nests.

From out of the wagon in which they traveled the last stretch, the children cried out joyfully to everyone they passed, "We're back, we're back again!"

A peasant harrowing in the fields pulled his horses up so short that their collars slid up to their heads, and waved his hat cheerfully in the air. Women cutting grass on the edge of the field stood up and curtsied awkwardly. "Are you coming home at last? We thought we'd never see you again," said a small, bent woman with long arms. And a slender, very pretty one pulled her kerchief over her eyes, put her hands on her hips, and doubled over with laughter for pure delight. The school had just spit out its entire contents of male and female pupils. A deafening clamor arose, caps flew in the air, and at the gate of the little courtyard a great crowd formed. The catechist shot out of the door as though out of the barrel of a gun and into the midst of the noisy troop. With a practiced hand he distributed slaps right and left, meanwhile bowing most deferentially to the master and mistress.

Hermann ordered the driver to stop, a few words were exchanged, the whole school was invited for the following Sunday to a children's party in the park, and the carriage drove on. A one-year volunteer from the twelfth regiment of the dragoons had accompanied them on horseback since their arrival at the train station. A tall, handsome fellow, blond, blue-eyed, and with the face of a good-natured child. It was Willi, Wilhelm's oldest son, on a powerful bay horse, a present from Hermann.

The young man had passed his examinations brilliantly the year before, was stationed now in the neighborhood, and would come under his father's strict supervision in the fall, when he would begin to rise through the ranks on the family farm. It would fall to him to step in for his father if the ability of the latter to support his family were, sooner or later, to fail. And not only to support them, but to keep them prosperous, according to Wilhelm's definition. His children had always left the table full; each of the eight scamps had been offered the opportunity to learn, to begin early to take the course to which his inclinations and his talents directed him. And the originator of the ability to offer them so much was the good native soil, which yielded all that a faithful son and caretaker might ask of it.

In difficult times, which the farmer is not spared, Wilhelm had occasionally had to accept his cousin's help, always offered with ingenious tact. But Wilhelm did it so reluctantly that Hermann lost his patience every time.

"What is the meaning of this? You're insulting me . . . . He accepts my brotherly love, yes, but my wretched pennies — oh, God forbid, no, not those! There he protests. Why, I'd like to know, why?"

"Because I don't like people to whom I owe something," answered Wilhelm, and his face grew purple. "I don't like them, confound it, I mean what I say! When someone props me up, I feel like a little boy. That's the way I am. Change me if you can."

That, of course, Hermann could not do, and Wilhelm's kindness and good nature returned only once he had paid back the debt he owed to his nearest relative and best friend. Yes, he was incorrigible, and Hermann was not one to preach in the desert or, indeed, to preach at all. If there was anything that aroused his scorn, it was the tendency to pedantry that animates most people, which they, however, disguise as a virtue and pass off as interest or sympathy. Hermann was unable to censure a failing in those dear to him even when it caused him suffering.

He therefore kept silent for a long time about the fact that Maria conspicuously neglected her adorable second son in favor of the older, independent one who was bursting with vigor, and hid from her his pained surprise at every sign of the disparity in her feelings for the children.

Perhaps she did not realize it. Perhaps she was unaware that there was a change in her entire manner when she turned from one child to the other. But if she was unaware of it, why did it happen that Maria seemed to regard the affection that was occasionally wrung from her by the little one as a theft perpetrated against her firstborn, for which she then attempted to compensate him a hundredfold?

He at last did ask her about it, and her answer was a glance so painfully disconcerted that Hermann thought, "She does reproach herself for her injustice, she is certainly struggling against the emotion that drives her to it, and she will also be victorious."

Around this time, Fée, who had recently established herself at Dornach in Aunt Dolph's wake, moved over to the Wonsheims. "Magnificent people over there," she said, "but they bore you to death. Nothing but the Wilhelm family, nothing but harmony, nothing but love, which isn't even a love one has anything to do with. No, thank you!"

The brothers suggested that it might be "downright practical" if they were once again to "stir things up." The attempt they made met with little favor, however. It soon became apparent that the most amusing person at Dornach was, at the moment, "old Dolph." She at least had the appropriate passion for lawn tennis, the only sport that the now dull neighbors had not stopped cultivating. Her headaches plagued her far more in the country than in the city; among all the things that she disliked, drafts were prominent on the list; yet, with tennis, she could hold out for hours in the role of a referee, of a rigorously strict "umpire."

"Because it gives her the chance to torment people," thought Miss Ninnemann.

When the Wonsheim party drove over in their "stagecoach" to Dornach for a game, they often had to submit to unflattering attention from the ignorant populace. The gentlemen in their high white felt hats, white juggler's suits, and white string gloves, the ladies wrapped up in pinafores like the little blacksmiths from Demavend, the bib decorated with garishly colored heraldic emblems, were often mistaken for a band of tightrope-walkers.

Naturally they were, one and all, such skilled tennis players that they could have played the English game. Hermann and Maria were almost as good, and there were sets that seemed endless. Even the opponents had to admire one other; only the "umpire" could never be quite satisfied.

Although a ball might be served over the net with incomparable grace and mathematical precision, be picked up with almost invariable assurance, and although it often flew back and forth thirty times before it fell to the ground, Aunt Dolph would deign to bestow only qualified praise.

"Quite good, children; not bad at all for a local game. Abroad you would be snubbed. Shout all you like; I can't help you. Just recently I had a visit from a Miss Nieuwenhuis-Kabeljau, the world's leading female tennis player. She wears a size 6 1/2 glove on her left hand, a size 8 glove on her right, and is as lop-sided as a barge about to tip over, I tell you, from all that racket-swinging. That's what I call practice, and it's the only way to acquire perfection."

"And a hunchback," Fée replied. "That might make me think twice."

"Amateur! That *juffrouw*[29] is prouder of it than a hero of his scars."

"And has every reason to be," declared Betty Wonsheim, examining her right hand and flattering herself inwardly, "Somewhat larger than the left one, sure enough, thank goodness."

Before the departure of the guests, plans were made to meet again the following afternoon for a party in the woods. Countess Dolph was giving it on Assumption Day.[30]

She found it necessary to show her gratitude for the many courtesies already extended her in the neighborhood. "My invitation to a little 'diversion,' as we used to say in Vienna, is nothing but payback, my dear Wilhelms and Wonsheims; it is supposed to give you back a small part of the pleasure your kindness has already given me."

Young and old expected wonders. The party in the woods (Fée had wormed the secret out of the good Ninnemann) was only a pretext to draw Hermann and Maria away from the manor for a while. On their return a grand surprise would await them: a magical illumination of the house and the garden, and fireworks directed by Stuwer himself.

The time and place of the rendezvous were set. They decided to meet at four o'clock in the afternoon at the former fowling floor.[31] Most of them wanted to take a detour through the woods and climb to the ruins first. Aunt Dolph and Helmi announced that they would stay with the children, who, with their attendants, would be sent directly to the "owl house."

It was their favorite place in the forest and was reachable in half an hour by carriage. The abandoned fowler's hut, overgrown with vines, always aroused great interest on Hermann and Erich's part. They rattled the locked door and, with fervent curiosity and light, delicious shudders, peeked through the tiny windows that were almost blinded by wire netting. Those who looked very long and very carefully, those who caught the right moment, when the wind moved the branches of the trees and a ray of sunlight could penetrate through the fissured roof into the dark room, would see something: the remains of an oven and of a larking-glass, nets gnawed by mice, a weasel that whisked from one hole in the wall to another, and, on a rotting perch, an owl. And the malevolent bird of prey had only one wing left and one glass eye, and that eye was terrifying and flashed yellow whenever a ray of light glided over it . . . . Oh, the hut under the alders concealed amazing things! But, thank heavens, there was no longer any danger there to finches and titmice and robins, and whatever they are called, the little warblers. Now they could alight safely on the small branches, which bobbed up and down under their delicate burden. Sing, twitter, rejoice, and then soar up again to pierce the air and return to your young. You need no longer fear death or imprisonment.

The hut was in a beautiful location, surrounded by woodland, and with a view only to the east. There a green meadow spread out, and yonder shimmered the broad, clear stream that later, narrowed by rocky reefs, fell into the gorge as a torrent. The ancient fortified castle looked down upon it from one of the moss-covered rocky giants. Even now, in its decay, it rose up proud and commanding.

The Wonsheims had already driven off when Miss Ninnemann appeared, tired and harassed. She had been to the post office twice, had exchanged nine telegrams with Sacher and Demel by order of her countess, and had just received the assurance that everything ordered had been sent and would arrive punctually the next day. When she learned that a group would be going to the ruins, she announced that she wanted to participate.

"I have longed for some time to visit the castle," she said to her mistress. "You know my fondness for the Middle Ages."

"Why don't you say, 'my gushing infatuation'? You imagine it all so poetically, the way the noble knights, their helmet plumes waving, fell upon the traveling merchants, struck them dead, and robbed them. The way they burned and ravished the land, stole the farmer's horses from his very plow, and flayed him when he tried to resist. The way they destroyed the houses of their weaker neighbors, hung their wives on the doorpost, kidnapped their daughters — if they were pretty, of course — and took them to their infamous . . . ahem . . ." she cleared her throat. "Perhaps you, too, would have been kidnapped and taken away, Ninny."

"Countess," interrupted the latter, "I will not permit — "

"Ha! You would have permitted all of it. You would have embroidered scarves for your raven-haired knight and sat at his side, cultivating romantic love, in front of the castle dungeon, from which the moans of the prisoners rotting on rotten straw would have penetrated to your ears."

Miss Ninnemann rose. "That is enough, Countess; in fact, it is even too much."

"There we have it; she's offended now," sighed Dolph. "You shouldn't gush over the age of chivalry, my dear. Your heart is too thin-skinned for that."

That night heard many fervent prayers from Dornach and its surroundings.

"Dear God," Fée pleaded, kneeling before her bed, "dear God, You know everything; You also know that Aunt Dolph got a letter today from Tessin. Dear God, let it say, 'I've always had a soft spot in my heart for the little one, and I want to marry her.'"

"Dear God," murmured Miss Ninnemann, tying on her nightcap and pulling her blanket up over her ears, "dear God, holy Virgin, holy martyrs, give me patience with my countess." She went still further and asked even to be able to feel some love for her tormenter. But this request was considered imprudent, even in heaven, and was disregarded.

The evening prayers of the youngest members of Wilhelm's household proved to be ardent. Six-year-old Rudi articulated it: "You are so good to children, dear God; because You are so good, dear God, let there be nice weather tomorrow."

Until late at night, the heat had been oppressive; now a cool northerly breeze arose, first gently, then stronger and stronger. There was a rustling in the treetops, a wild confusion of all sorts of voices; the branches groaned and laughed and uttered loud cries. "Relief, relief!" whispered the swaying boughs. Voluminous clouds that had hung comfortably on the horizon rose up suddenly from their repose. Transformed first from thick knots into long strands, they flitted away at last, quite thin and transparent.

The moon stood high in the sky in undisputed splendor as Willi approached his parents' home several hours past midnight. He walked his horse across the paved courtyard. In the low, shingled stables on either side of it, both people and animals were still sleeping. A dog that lay curled up on a threshold growled in its dreams. Then all fell silent once more; even the little fountain in front of the so-called castle had ceased its splashing. That grieved the young soldier. He had bought a lovely new stone basin for it with the extra money his Uncle Hermann had given him. And now the fountain had run dry. "The water pipes have gone bad again," he said to himself, "and there's no money to repair them."

Poor little fountain; poor, beloved paternal home! With its bare walls, narrow arched windows, and steep, uneven roof, even the transfiguring moonlight could not make it pretty. Its only ornament was a wooden balcony, whose sagging posts and wobbly railing hid themselves under lushly growing wild vines.

Willi tapped gently at the door in order to wake only the gardener who also served as doorkeeper, gave him his horse, and entered.

The next morning his brothers shouted with joy as they greeted a day of unprecedented magnificence, and they knew quite well for whose sake it had been sent.

At Dornach, little Hermann ran from father to mother and then from mother to father. He could not sit still and was charming in his eagerness and his impatience. "You know, Erich," he said, hugging him impetuously, "today we'll stay up as late as the grown-ups. We're going to the owl."

"And what will you do there?" Aunt Dolph asked.

"I'm going to look."

"And then?"

"And then I'll run, I'll run in the meadow, so fast that no one will see me, as fast — " he opened his eyes wide, raised his arms over his head, and struggled to find an appropriately extreme comparison, "as fast — "

"As the devil," his aunt came to his aid, but he made a gesture of disdain and said, "Oh, much faster than that!"

She patted him on the cheek, laughing; she who did not like children, because they made noise and left doors open, had a soft spot for this grandnephew. "A true child of the aristocracy," she declared. "From pure and healthy stock; well-fed, well-housed, and well-washed from the first breath he took; doesn't know what fear is, or miserliness; can deal a blow, if necessary, and will, if necessary, give away the shirt off his back. Courage, kindness, generosity — he has all the virtues I lack — that's why I love him."

Miss Ninnemann stared at her, bewildered, and thought, "Strange, she never had a heart before; has she suddenly grown one?"

XVII.

At the edge of the pine forest, through which a wide path led to the ruins, Hermann and Maria, accompanied by Miss Ninnemann, met the Wonsheims, with Fée, and Wilhelm, with Willi and the next two in line. A couple of sturdy farm horses had done the latter the favor of carrying them here in a gallop that shook the earth under their feet.

The ladies had already hopped out of the carriage; Wilhelm and his sons had dismounted. Only Gustav and Clemens were still on horseback and were conferring with their wives, who had found it necessary to come dressed as tourists. They wore lightweight hats with blue veils, short dresses made of summer wool, laced boots of Russia leather, thick goat's hair stockings, and, over their shoulders, pale yellow mackintoshes of rubberized cotton cloth.

"Look here, Countess," said Clemens to Maria, not without secret pride, "see how they've gotten themselves up. And the things they come up with — now they want to climb the mountain by way of the crumbling footpath."

"Because one has such a beautiful view from there," said Carla.

"And because it's dangerous," Betty chimed in.

"And so poetic, isn't that right, Miss Ninnemann? That would be something for you," Fée joked good-naturedly. "I offer you my arm; I'll get you up there, I swear it!"

Miss Ninnemann curtsied so low that it looked as though she wanted to sit down; dissolving into nervous gratitude, she accepted the kind proposition.

94

The driver with the carriage and the groom with the horses were sent on ahead to the meeting place. Wilhelm issued his orders in an unusually gruff tone, meanwhile grumbling to himself, "Foolishness! What cursed foolishness . . . choosing such a path . . . that was none other than Willi's idea . . . ."

"Lead on, soldier!" said the ladies, waved good-bye to those who were staying behind, and started on their way.

Wilhelm hesitated a moment; then he followed them in order to watch over his Willi. "The damned boy is hopping around as though he were on springs; he seems to be paying court — and to three at once. Just you wait, young fellow, I'm not leaving your side."

"And what will you do, Countess?" asked Gustav.

"I'll go on foot too, but with the good path," Maria answered cheerfully and took her husband's arm.

"Then we'll ride ahead slowly." And they set off on their famous black thoroughbreds.

"They've all taken off. Is there anyone more impolite than our guests?" Hermann joked.

"*We* are; we let them go without trying to stop them."

"And are left to ourselves, which is the best thing there is," he began again after a short pause. "When I think that there are people who can say, 'Love fades away,' and yet believe they have known love, the fools! Mine is the same today as it was in the first hour I saw you and knew nothing about you but your name."

He held her close; side by side they walked on. The riders had disappeared from sight; a sublime solitude reigned, a magically animated tranquillity. Fiery sunlight floated above the treetops, and cool shadows undulated at their feet. The forest seemed to spread out immeasurably, a holy, consecrated place that, when entered by lovers, frees them from obtrusive thoughts of the outside world, from the awareness of the passing of time.

Maria had disengaged herself gently from Hermann; she stepped in front of him and looked earnestly into his eyes. "I, however," she began suddenly, "love you more every day. And *my* love — *sees*."

"In contrast to mine, which presumably is blind?"

"Undeniably," she responded and pulled him toward her.

At this he cried out, "Long live my blind love! The night with which it surrounds me is like no other: it is dazzlingly light. It shows me the benevolent spirit of my house, she who comforts the melancholy — "

"And so on," she interrupted him with forced laughter. "Stop that, Hermann, I beg you — "

"All right, then, no, not a word in your praise. But how shall I begin to keep silent about what fills my heart? You ask me to pretend? You, who are ever and always truthful?" He seized her hands; they trembled in his. "What upsets you so? Tell your best friend . . . . You see, sometimes — I'll confess this to you —

sometimes, when you avoid my gaze, when you shiver at my touch, as you are doing now, it seems as though your soul were concealing a secret, a mysterious emotion, a painful memory — I don't know what. Is that an illusion, Maria, foolishness, a crime against you? Answer me."

She stood as though turned to stone. Her regal figure upright, her head raised as though she were offering it up to a flash of lightening, hardly breathing, her eyes lowered, an unspoken word on her faintly quivering lips.

And she was beautiful in that solemn motionlessness, with the humbly proud expression of a tortured saint.

The man who worshipped her stared at her, ashamed and remorseful. Had he not expressed suspicion of her in the question he had long suppressed and now thrown at her so thoughtlessly?

"And if you were right?" Maria said, in a tone that was as harsh and strangled as though it were cutting her throat in two.

"About what? You have misunderstood me — "

"Suppose that I had done you a wrong," she continued, with difficulty, in the same stifled voice, "suppose it."

"*What* should I suppose — the impossible? I would first have to go mad . . . ." He struck his forehead with his fist. "I don't understand you — why this unnecessary cruelty? What horrible test are you putting me to?"

"Test?" she repeated. "Would your love pass that test, the most difficult, most dreadful . . . . And if it had happened — what I spoke of — what would you do?"

She kept her eyes fixed upon the ground and only felt him put his hand firmly on her arm.

And now he spoke, and his voice had its deep, gentle tone once again, and his words came from the inexhaustible well of his kindness, "If that had happened, which you are not even able to name, then what gives my life value would have been taken from me. But I would love you still, and to this unconquerable love would be added a limitless sorrow: I know you and I know that you would be destroyed by the awareness of your guilt."

Oh, this faith, as strong and as true as the heart that cherished it, the heart she had wanted to break in order to relieve her own! "You must not!" cried a voice within her. "You have deceived — you must lie! You have forfeited your right to truth."

"Come," Hermann said, seating himself on a moss-covered stone, half sunken in the soft soil of the forest. "You must first rest and become cheerful again before we follow the others. There's a wonderful velvet cushion spread out here just for us. Come to me!"

"Here I am," she said and sank down in front of him, folded her hands on his knee, and leaned against his chest. "Let me look up to you in humility; it does me good."

"We've been tormenting one another, and it was completely my fault with my foolish brooding," he said. "Forgive me!"

"I — forgive you? My friend, my angel, if you would only once give me a chance to do so! Do it, please. Let me experience the bliss of being able to forgive you for something."

"I thank you for your excellent intention," he cried with comic dismay. "I will give you the opportunity to put it into practice — at least I will try."

"You will fail." She put her arms around him and clasped her fingers behind his neck. "Look at me; your eyes are like your soul. Look at me with that gaze of benediction. How devout I am! The forest has become a temple, and I am a wretched mortal, and you are the priest whose strong hand leads me to salvation."

XVIII.

There was already brisk activity at the ruins when Hermann and Maria approached. Miss Ninnemann, who looked redder than ever and was literally swollen from the heat, was the first to catch sight of them.

"There they are, there is the charming couple," she cried. "I ask you to contemplate the count. 'It is lovely to descry / how the suns of his heart set in his eye.' And how much he, as always, looks like the image we have of the heroic Siegfried!"

"Yes, indeed, there is something to that, except that his wife is not Kriemhild, but Isolde,"[32] said Fée and ran to meet the new arrivals. Hermann and Maria soon found themselves in the company of their merry guests, with whom they could marvel at the exploits to which Willi had been inspired by the presence of three young and beautiful ladies.

Just now he was strolling from one tower battlement to another along a beam that had been installed to support them. His brothers, spurred on by his example, scrambled like cats up the old walls.

Wilhelm stood below and clenched his fists. "All my boys have the devil in them when it comes to showing off to a female audience," he said to Hermann. "Not a good trait at all. Ladies' men are cut from such cloth."

Hermann clapped him on the back and said, "You don't even believe that yourself, old fellow," and the Wonsheims smiled and watched the boys' reckless ventures with the air of guardian angels. Betty lamented that she had not been born a man, which was the only good thing to be. Miss Ninnemann wallowed in rapture, ignoring the fact that her colorful muslin dress had suffered greatly during the "ascension," and rebuilt the entire fortified castle in her mind — the ruined surrounding wall rose from the ground and encircled, as in times past, the gates, the bailey, the drawbridge, and the bohort field, where knights in armor had jousted; she restored the entrance and the steps that led up to the magnificent "palace."

97

Carla and Gustav, both of whom she assured that the *"dames châtelaines"* would all have looked like the blond Countess Wonsheim, listened to her attentively. Gustav marveled at so much "learning" and did not know whether he should admire it or find it ridiculous. Although he was convinced of the accuracy of each of Annette's assertions, he did not want to reveal that. Thus every time she paused he would say, "Oh, come on, now!"

"Ah, and this air! This ozone!" Miss Ninnemann enthused. "If I could only dwell here!"

"Dwell here all you like," replied Fée, who had joined the group. "But don't count on me for the climb. You slipped seventeen times — I counted. My right arm is almost broken because you clung to it like a drowning person. With all due respect, you're getting fat."

Miss Ninnemann drew in her breath and stretched her spine in order to look thinner. "If I'm putting on weight, then it's thanks to affliction and worry. That happens; yes, indeed — I am living proof of it," she said, not without bitterness.

Fée apologized, "Now, now, don't take offense."

The lady companion vowed that she would sooner die than take offense at something the countess had done, at which Fée hugged her and said, "You know, you're not spoiled, you dear old soul, you dear old Ninnikins."

In the meantime, Clemens had climbed out on a rocky ledge and called, pointing to the meadow on the other side of the stream, "Here you have it; here's a fine view of Aunt Dolph, and of your boys, Wilhelm, who are running around, and of the tea party."

"And of a rickety footbridge," Hermann interjected. "How often have I had that torn down; it's put back up every time, even now that the water is high."

"You won't be able to change that as long as they're felling trees in the mountains," said Wilhelm. "A woodcutter won't go the extra two hundred feet over the main bridge."

"I wouldn't do it either," Fée cried. "Especially if there were someone I particularly liked standing on the other side. But look, just look. The view is really worthwhile. Let's all enjoy it for the time being."

Everyone crowded around her. In the meadow several servants were preparing an unusually abundant "five o'clock tea" under Helmi's supervision. The greediest of the young gentlemen followed their activities very attentively, while the others attempted to view the curiosities hidden in the fowling floor.

Countess Dolph had kept her seat in the wagon, which had stopped at the shady edge of the forest. She was enjoying the demonstration of running skill that Hermann, her favorite, had promised. He ran to the willows at the far end of the meadow and back, this way and that, just like a colt giving full vent to its youthful vigor.

Suddenly he stopped, raised his head, looked up at the ruins, and, when he spied his parents up there on the mountain, held out his arms to them and blew kisses at them. "I see you, Father, Mother, you're so tiny," — he measured them against his finger — "so tiny!"

His voice did not reach them; they could see only his charming gestures as he approached the bank of the stream, they sang the praises of the "splendid boy," and waved to him. Clemens made a megaphone of his hands and called, "Come on up, if you're got the courage!"

Suddenly Maria cried out in alarm, and Hermann, leaning over the precipice, shouted with all his might, "Away from the water . . . go back!"

The child seemed to have made a quick decision and was running toward the footbridge. The elderly nurse, who had stayed close to him, ran after him, stumbling and wheezing.

The interest of the other children had been aroused. One and the same impulse shot through them all: follow Hermann to the footbridge. And away they flew, with Wilhelm's seven-year-old Hansel in the lead.

It took some time before Helmi, with the help of the nanny and the servants, was able to catch the fugitives. The nurse had just managed to seize Hermann as well; the resistance he put up seemed to have been overcome when, with a vigorous jerk, he suddenly succeeded in pulling away and escaping.

"I *do* have the courage! Father, Mother, I'm coming to you!" He ran and ran, and all those who came hurrying after him from the meadow were left far behind.

Then his little white tunic shimmered though the branches of the willows, and then he appeared on the footbridge.

At the same moment, Hermann rushed to the steep and rocky path and down its crumbling steps. Without a word, Maria followed him, and, swift as an arrow, Willi was at her side.

None of the others hesitated to take the dizzying path either. None of them thought of what they risked. *One* emotion filled them all, the same fear, the same wish. They slipped, they tottered, they caught their balance and ran on. For the length of a heartbeat they paused in their hazardous undertaking.

With light-hearted strides, the child had gotten to the middle of the footbridge, exulting loudly, and had challenged his pursuers, "Now try and catch me, just try!" He looked around, quickened his pace, stumbled, and fell.

Overtaking all the others, Hermann had reached the bank. Keeping his eyes fixed on the child, who, without sinking, was being swept away by the current, he threw off his coat and leapt into the turbulent water.

Wilhelm and Clemens had followed on his heels. The former was fully alert and knew what he wanted to do; the latter was half-crazed with horror at the consequences of his fateful joke. Wilhelm ran with lightning speed to the bridge. Next to it a boat had been pulled up on land; slender tree-trunks destined for the repair of the fowler's hut were piled up on it. Wilhelm reached for one of them but let it fall when Clemens discovered a rafter's pole that had either been forgotten or hidden in the boat. Quicker than words can describe, the two of them hurried back and arrived at the spot where Hermann, with superhuman strength, was holding out against the force of the current.

"Closer! For God's sake, closer!" he heard now, and Wilhelm and Clemens, each holding the pole tightly with both hands, stretched it toward him as far as they could. He tried to grasp it . . . . He missed.

Then Clemens jumped into the water, fought his way forward to the very end of the pole, which Wilhelm, with difficulty, now balanced alone, and made a desperate, futile attempt to rescue them. The enormous spiral of the whirlpool had already encircled father and son and pulled them down and with savage fury thrown them up again, gasping, covered with foam. A last, horrible struggle. Exhausted, overcome, flung mercilessly against the rocks, Hermann still attempted to cover his child's body with his own.

On both banks people press forward to the scene of the tragedy; on this side, those who had hurried after Hermann, and on the other, his servants, drivers, footmen, workers who had chanced to pass by. There is not one of them who does not want to help, who does not make a fervent attempt.

Only Maria, Hermann's name on her lips, gripped by the mad desire to follow him into his deadly peril, stood motionless. Her entire soul was in her eyes, opened unnaturally wide; in her gaze, as she stared after him. Suddenly it seemed to her as though night had fallen — her pulse faltered, she swayed, and lay in the arms of someone who held her tightly. Carla Wonsheim held her upright; Betty lay sobbing at her feet and clung to her knees. Someone prayed loudly; from a distance came the muddled sound of voices.

Waking out of her half-unconscious state, Maria hastened toward them. People, more and more people ran together. Some of them carried a heavy burden and then laid it down — oh, how gently and carefully . . . .

Suddenly it is as though the crowd had begun to stir joyfully. "The doctor!" cries a servant running toward them, out of breath. "The forester is bringing him; he was with his sick child."

All fell silent as Maria drew near. Everyone stepped back mutely before her. One man, half-undressed, dripping, approaches her; he writhes, whimpering and moaning. He clutches the hem of her dress.

"Trample me! I did it, I called him, I — accursed creature, as stupid as an animal — trample on my empty head, trample me to death!" he wailed and buried his face in the grass at her feet.

Maria stepped aside. She had caught sight of the lifeless figures, the gaping wound on Hermann's forehead, the pale face of her boy. She started back, wrung her hands and lifted them toward heaven, and sank to the ground with a terrible cry of anguish, "Dead? Both of them dead?"

No one answered; she gathered herself up and, bending over Hermann, covered his breast with her kisses and cried, "He's alive, Doctor! His heart is beating; I felt it!"

The doctor, who, although without any hope, had not yet given up attempting to revive the child, shook his head in answer. She, however, pressed her mouth to that of the dead man and breathed into it until her breath failed her. She did not arouse the slightest response from him. And now she understood that she had lost him. Again she threw herself upon him — but suddenly, braced against his shoulder, she lifted her head and cast a look of trembling dread at her son. "Him too?" she moaned, with a voice in which all the pain the human soul can comprehend seemed to be compressed. "My child too!"

Close to madness, she prayed, she begged for a miracle . . . .

When they returned home, those who had left the house cheerful and gay a few hours earlier were met by the sparkle of hundreds of thousands of small colored lamps. Resplendent in a sea of light, Castle Dornach received its dead master.

XIX.

Maria kept the first vigil alone with her dead. They had not been able to disengage the hand of the child from that of his father, and so the two of them lay next to each other on one bed and would lie in one coffin as well. Their pale faces bore no trace of that last difficult struggle. Maria held them both in her embrace. She lay clinging to them, as pale and mute as they but without their peace. She had only one consolation in her devastation, and she was conscious of it as she pressed her head against the silent heart whose joyous beating had brought her all her happiness.

Thank God she had spared him the worst, that his faith in her had been unshaken to the end. Thanks to that mysterious force that, every time she had wanted to speak, had driven the words that would have made him wretched back into her breast. Now he had gone to his eternal rest with a serene expression and a smile on his lips.

Lisette was in the next room, suppressing her sobs so that she would not be heard by her mistress and sent away. Once she had ventured to approach the door noiselessly and had peered through the keyhole.

Maria sat beside the bed, motionless, lost in the contemplation of her husband and son and with an expression of such heart-rending grief on her face that Lisette started back from the door. No, she could not bear that, she could not see that.

In the morning she finally knocked at the door and, when there was no answer, entered unbidden, called to her mistress, and said, "It is morning."

Maria started. "Already?"

"Yes, my poor child, and you must go. The gentlemen are here . . . you know — and Count Wilhelm."

He stood with Helmi at the door. His eyes were red and swollen; his lips quivered. He could not speak and leaned helplessly against his wife. The doctor

CARL A. RUDISILL LIBRARY
LENOIR-RHYNE COLLEGE

and Willi came, and behind them Erich entered shyly, holding a large bouquet of white roses in both hands.

"The gardener told me I should bring these to Hermann," he said to his mother. "Hermann, here they are."

He laid the flowers on the bed and, leaning on its edge, raised himself as high as he could, stretched forward, and puckered his lips to kiss his brother. But he could not reach him and asked, "Why didn't you sleep with me last night?" Now he saw his father, who also did not stir, whose eyes were also closed . . . .

Thoroughly dismayed, he stepped back. "Why are they sleeping so long?" he cried suddenly. "They should wake up, Mother, tell them that they should wake up."

Maria bent down to him and took him in her arms. The first tears she had cried since yesterday fell on the head of her little son.

*   *   *

Wilhelm himself brought Countess Agathe the news of the terrible loss she had suffered. Helmi's pleas persuaded him to do it. She wanted him away from the scene of the tragedy, wanted to compel him to master his anguish by performing a difficult duty.

He returned earlier than they had expected. He had traveled day and night, partly by train, partly carried by farm horses, and he announced that the countess would be arriving the next morning, the day of the funeral.

"How did you find her?" Maria asked, looking away.

"Incomprehensible — she is either a saint or a stone," Wilhelm replied and related how the countess had been at church when he arrived at Dornachtal at nine o'clock in the morning. Her new confessor, a tall, stern-looking young man, received him and listened with cold surprise to his tragic tidings. He had not known the count; he had only heard about him. At that moment, Wilhelm hated him; in the next, he could have embraced him, because he offered to prepare the old lady for the news of the misfortune that had befallen her. Wilhelm waited in the room of the priest, who was to send for him when it was time. A half hour later he was called. Good, merciful God! She sat calmly in a high-backed armchair, the priest on a chair next to her, his eyes lowered, a triumphant smile on his thin lips. The countess, white as a sheet, held a rosary between her now lifeless-looking fingers.

"Thank you," she said, "for taking the trouble to come yourself." Then she asked him to tell Maria to expect her and requested that he not linger any longer, because she knew how necessary his presence was at Dornach. Her carriage, which would bring him to the train station after breakfast, stood ready.

Not a word about her son, about her grandson. Only when Wilhelm took his leave did she ask about Erich and whispered, with a grateful glance toward heaven, "God has left me him!"

At these words Maria started and buried her face in her hands.

Count Wolfsberg arrived shortly after Wilhelm, bent and aged. Few people could boast of being loved by the count; he had loved the two who would be buried tomorrow. But the change that had taken place in his daughter also moved and disturbed him. He watched her incessantly and anxiously, proved himself helpful, and aided her in her sorrowful service to the dead. Once he suddenly pulled her close, as tenderly as he had on the day before she left her paternal home. "You must live," he said. "You still have a task in this world."

She raised her eyes to him and answered with determination, "Yes, Father, yes!"

*　*　*

Wolfsberg and Maria awaited Countess Agathe under the portal. She descended from the carriage and, after a silent greeting, mounted the stairs, refusing any assistance. There she went directly to the chapel, where, for centuries, the counts of Dornach had found their final rest.

The room, trimmed in black, was filled with wailing, sobbing people. When the old lady entered, it was as though an icy wind had blown through the room. The tears stopped flowing; not another whimper was heard.

The countess attended the funeral holding herself upright and with majestic resignation evident in her stern features. Rigid in her grief, she uttered no complaint and did not ask for a description of the event that had robbed her of her son and grandson. "The Lord giveth and the Lord taketh away; blessed be the name of the Lord," was all that she said to comfort herself and her daughter-in-law. She added, however, "A common sorrow unites those who bear it." She let Maria know that the beloved wife of her son remained dear to her even after his death.

Aunt Dolph had disappeared during the past few days. Dr. Weise had had to prescribe complete rest and a change of air for her. Something unusual was going on inside her: when she thought of little Hermann she was seized by melancholy — not violently so, but it was worrisome enough for the old egotist, as an indisposition would be for someone who had always been healthy. She confessed it to her brother and also did not conceal from him her slight resentment of Maria, whose misfortune demanded pity — an uncomfortable sensation for the countess.

"I was put on earth to enjoy life with others, not to suffer with them. Why should the sadness spread? I'm going to get out of its way. If others find it abominable of me, I must reconcile myself to that. Can I help my nature? The vine weeps; the thistle doesn't," she said and departed.

There was, however, one happy creature in the sorely afflicted household that she abandoned. That was Erich; he wandered around as blissfully as someone who had returned from banishment to the longed-for paradise of home. His mother loved him now, the way she loved poor Hermann, who still had to sleep all the time. She lifted him up on her lap and overwhelmed him with tenderness.

And the child, joyfully surprised, a little disconcerted, submitted to this abundant love with quiet rapture.

Once she took him with her into the crypt and knelt before the recess, hung with wreaths, that held the coffin of her husband and her firstborn son.

"Erich," she said, taking both of his little hands into her own hands, "you will grow up one day and will be good and clever. You should think then of your mother and of what she says to you today."

The little one leaned his forehead against her cheek. "What does she say?"

"Look around you. Where are we?"

"In the crypt."

"And who is sleeping in the crypt?"

"My father and my brother."

"And many, many other good people who are related to them. Remember, Erich, don't forget this, remember, when you are grown up, where and when your mother said to you, 'Forgive me, my child, forgive me!' Will you remember that, child?"

Erich threw his arms around her neck and answered firmly and confidently, "Erich will remember it."

When they returned to the manor house, Wolfsberg came to meet them. "It is time," he said to Maria. "Your mother-in-law and Wilhelm are waiting for you. If you are not strong enough, however — "

Maria interrupted him, "I have sought strength and found it." She gave the boy to the nurse, who was waiting for him, and went with her father to the countess's chambers.

Before the funeral the will of the deceased had been opened in Wilhelm's and Wolfsberg's presence with the usual formalities. Its primary contents constituted a tribute to Maria, and Wolfsberg had hesitated to communicate the deeply affecting text of this last message to her. Today, the third day after Hermann had been laid to his eternal rest, the will would be read to her. Hermann's mother had expressed the wish to be present.

The countess received Maria and Wolfsberg in the drawing room of her widow's apartment in the manor. It was a high-ceilinged room with pale yellow stuccoed walls, large marble fireplaces, mirrors that reached to the ceiling in carved gilt frames, and stiff Empire[33] furnishings. The windows, from which one had an extensive view of the park, stood open; the light of the setting sun and the fragrant air from the forest entered through them.

The old lady in black, trailing garments, with an ash-grey face on which the suffering and inner struggles of the last few days were deeply etched, formed a somber contrast to this inviting room. She partially rose from her sofa corner as Maria came toward her, and, as she did so, she knocked a little cage with a stuffed bird to the floor. Before anyone else could do it for her, she bent down and picked it up and put the toy back where it had been. "Erich brought it in," she said, "and forgot it when you sent for him."

Maria clasped the hand the countess gave her, bowed deeply, kissed it ardently and sincerely, and brought it again and again to her lips, as though a painful parting were imminent.

"Now, now, my child," the countess admonished her, "compose yourself, I beg of you. We want to listen resolutely — as true believers — to the words of the dear one who has gone before us."

In the meantime Wilhelm had sat there silently, immersed in the document he was to read.

"Begin," said the countess.

He moved his chair closer to her. Maria had seated herself opposite him. Her father sat down next to her.

Wilhelm read in a low, agitated voice, and the elderly listener next to him was gradually overcome by a feeling she had not had for a long time, a gentle and melancholy emotion.

Many years ago, someone who had never been forgotten had spoken of her in his will the way Hermann spoke of the woman he loved. He had honored her with the same confidence by having given her as much power over the son, as much freedom in the administration of the estate as the law would allow. In nearly the same words as his father, Hermann wrote, "Because I have the true well-being of my children at heart, I submit them in every respect to their mother's decisions. In so doing, I commend them to a care that is wise, just, and faithful."

A tortured moan escaped Maria's breast.

Wilhelm stopped.

"Go on," said the countess, after a short pause.

In a choked voice, he continued to read and from time to time stole a glance at Maria. She was wringing her hands in her lap; her features, pale as marble, expressed inconsolable despair.

Wilhelm had come to the end. The conclusion was as follows: "The better and more capable my children become, and the more clearly they are able to judge the world and others, the deeper the conviction will take root in them that there is on earth a wisdom and a goodness above all others — and that it is embodied in their mother.

"I am glad to be alive, and I hope to live a long time and to be able to give my sons counsel in the future. But to you, Maria, whether I die young or old, to you I will always have only one thing to say: I thank you!"

Countess Agathe's eyes had reddened slightly; she turned to Maria with sympathy. The woman who had possessed and lost such a love was dear to her and would always be dear to her. "My daughter," she said to her, "I share my Hermann's belief. His most precious legacy, his beloved child, is safe in your care. God strengthen you and bless our little heir." She extended her right hand to place it on Maria's head.

The latter leapt up. "What are you doing? I don't deserve it. Treat me as I deserve to be treated," she cried passionately, faltered a moment, and then added in a harsh tone, "Erich is unfit to be the heir."

"Maria!" cried the others. The same thought had occurred to all of them.

"No, no, I have not gone mad; I know what I am saying. I can no longer endure the lie. The one for whose sake I did it is dead."

Beside himself, Wolfsberg grasped her shoulder with an iron hand. "Did what?"

"Dissembled — allowed myself to be taken for what I was not: faithful."

He pushed her away from him and jumped up; the countess, too, was standing, drawn up to her full height.

"Unfaithful? A Dornach unfaithful? No, not a Dornach. You are not of our blood — adulteress!" she flung at Maria and touched her handkerchief involuntarily to her mouth, which to her seemed sullied after uttering the word. "Erich not the son of my son . . . and I — and I!" With a short, shrill laugh, she sank back into the cushions, half-fainting, mute and rigid.

"You are lying, Maria!" cried Wilhelm. Shaking with fury, Wolfsberg stepped in front of his daughter. "Your excuse?" he snarled at her.

She looked calmly into his eyes, which flashed angrily; her own expressed more a reproach than an apology. "I had managed to save myself through my own strength," she could have answered. "Then the hand of your son brought me to ruin."

"Your excuse?" he cried again, this time in a lower voice, more urgently, disconcerted by her astounding composure. "You have an excuse."

"None," she replied.

"Impossible," Wilhelm interrupted. "If you did wrong, then an angel would have done wrong, and — " Suddenly he stopped.

The door next to the sofa had opened. Erich came out of Countess Agathe's room — and ran to her. "Grandmother, where is the little bird?" he asked and laid his crossed arms on her knees.

A last spark of love for this sweet child glimmered in her heart; she looked at him with sympathy, and then she ordered him away.

He, however, demanded impatiently, "The little bird, Grandmother, give it to me!" and clung to her.

Then she shook him off, as though something unclean had touched her. "Get out!" she commanded harshly. Her face was distorted; her hands were clenched convulsively. "Get out!"

Erich, astonished, dismayed, blushed deeply; the corners of his mouth turned down; he still looked sideways for the birdcage and fought to keep back the sobs they could hear as soon as he had left the room.

Maria remained motionless. Her cousin Wilhelm watched her in unutterable suspense and longed for her to speak and take back the slander she had uttered against herself . . . . For what reason? With what intention? . . . His thoughts whirled around in his feverish head; his fiery temples pounded. Desperately seeking coolness, he went to the window.

The balmy air wafted toward him and wakened a whispering sound in the treetops. Swallows circled the house. With a beating of wings, white doves rose up from the capital of a column and dissolved into the blue like tiny flakes.

"Wilhelm!"

He turned around; the countess had called his name.

"The old Dornach line has died out," she said solemnly and turned pale with the impression that her own words made on her. "May God protect its younger branch and, above all, you, its head."

He staggered backwards. "Me . . . me?"

"You are the next in line. Is that news to you?" asked Wolfsberg, bitterly.

"I will not lay claim to it, never!"

"As though you had a choice."

"You will do what is your duty and what you must do," said the countess.

"Must?" he responded with vehemence. "And what has just been said here *must* be revealed to the world, and the law *must* give its blessing to the declaration that has been made — " He stopped; a possibility of salvation had flashed through his mind. "The law will *not* give its blessing! According to the law, a child born in wedlock is legitimate and its inheritance cannot be disputed."

Countess Agathe started up. "*Its* inheritance? The law? There is a law that protects the child of sin when it stretches out its hand toward other people's property?"

"Don't let that worry you!" Wolfsberg interrupted. He had grown pale; beads of sweat glistened on his forehead. "The child will never touch Dornach property; he will be raised as befits him, and once he is of age he will sign his renunciation of the title with the awareness that the act of signing is a mere formality. I guarantee it."

"And I," said Maria, and Wilhelm cried, completely beside himself, "And you! Then you will be delivering yourself up to slander. Have you thought of that?"

With a cheerless smile, she said, "Dear Wilhelm, surely you don't want to protect me — a guilty party who has been more than convicted, who has confessed. For years I have endured love and reverence while conscious of my worthlessness. That was more difficult."

"Words, empty words," the countess responded, stiffly and pitilessly. "If it had pleased God to spare my son, you would have continued living in falsehood and deceit."

"Not much longer," Maria asserted gently and movingly, "believe me. The smallest concession granted to the — the illegitimate child would have loosened my tongue, and then I would have stood before Hermann, as I now stand before his mother, and would have asked — " Her voice became almost inaudible. "May I bid you farewell?"

A dismissive gesture was the countess's answer; Wilhelm, however, went to Maria and said reproachfully, "Farewell? You want to leave us? What can you be thinking of? We love you — you are like a daughter to my Helmi. Stay with us. Come live with us in our modest house. Stay with us!" He clapped himself on the chest. "You have a friend who honors you and who will repeat even with his dying breath, 'Where she has sinned, even an angel would have fallen.'"

Maria clasped his hand gratefully. "We will see each other again," she uttered with difficulty, "at Wolfsberg, where my father will give shelter to me and the child. Isn't that right, Father?"

"I am never going back to Wolfsberg," he replied harshly. In this hour his love for her belied itself.

"Maria!" cried Wilhelm, "we will bless every day you give us. Stay with us!"

"It cannot be — you will see that," she said. Her cheeks had flushed slowly and now glowed feverishly.

For the second time she turned to her father. "Nevertheless, take us in!"

He shrugged his shoulders and answered, "What else can I do?"

XX.

The ancestral Castle Wolfsberg was a bulky stone structure with gloomy arched halls, damp corridors, and walls four feet thick. The count had once gone to great expense to make it habitable and had had one part of it furnished in an old-fashioned style, while the other part was intended to meet all of the demands that are made nowadays on the country homes of wealthy and hospitable people. Later, after the death of his wife, he regretted the romantic whim that had led him to take up residence in a dreary and uninviting region, in the vicinity of a village populace to which all the vices of poverty clung. He left Dolph and Maria alone at Wolfsberg for months at a time; his visits there became shorter and shorter, and after his daughter was married he gave them up entirely.

The castle rose from a truncated hill, which at the beginning of the century had still been densely wooded. An ancestor in need of money had had the trees felled and had not reforested the land. Gullies had formed, the fertile soil had been washed away by heavy showers, and the clayey sandstone that had come to light was gradually covered by sparse vegetation. Here and there the scarred and crooked trunk of a pine tree with clusters of gray-green needles on its dry branches jutted out of the stone, and wherever a tiny spring trickled, there was luxuriant moss. The roots of the ancient oaks that stood in front of the gatehouse had sent out runners, which decorated themselves with leaves. Harebells and various heathers grew out of the debris.

Thanks to the abundance of trees in the manor garden, the ground water did not dry up entirely. Within the garden's rambling, many-angled surrounding wall, which in some places extended halfway down the hill, there was an expanse of splendid meadowland, and in the village there was even talk of flowers and of hothouses where the flowers passed the winter. There was no communication between the village and the manor. Hostility had reigned between the two ever since the community had rewarded the count's first acts of charity with ingratitude. Each side found fault with the other on every possible occasion.

While honoring the memory of the deceased mistress of the manor, the people conferred their deepest hatred upon the count, in whose spirit the stewards of the estate conducted their business with the village. A mixture of truth and malicious invention had been preserved as tradition in the region. No one doubted that the countess had succumbed to the maltreatment she had suffered from her husband and that now her spirit wandered through the corridors, creeping to his door and listening. One night he had seen her ghostly eye peering through the keyhole. Now this eye followed him everywhere and stared at him from every corner of the house. It was no wonder that he could not bear to be at Wolfsberg; it was no wonder that his insolent servants gradually began to act as though they were the masters of his property.

The count's telegram, which announced that Maria would be arriving for a long stay, dethroned half a dozen usurpers with one blow and unleashed a storm of angry questions: "What business does she have coming here? Why doesn't she stay where she belongs?"

Welcomed by no one, Maria returned to her childhood home with Erich and her small entourage.

The wind-blown locust trees lining the avenue that led to the manor house; the tiny chapel dedicated to the Virgin Mary at the foot of the hill, surrounded by four linden trees; the broad view of the fields and the pastures and the dark pine forest in the background, a view that one achieved upon ascending the hill and that extended as far as the quarry — she had loved all of that. And how barren, how utterly melancholy it seemed to her now!

"Where are the meadows? Where are the mountains?" cried Erich, looking out the window the morning after their arrival. He went into the village with Lisette and returned full of indignation. "They have very bad manners here," he related. "They don't answer when you say 'Good morning,' and a boy," he lowered his voice and whispered in his mother's ear, "stuck out his tongue at me."

"They don't know you yet," she responded. "Just wait; soon they'll be as friendly to you as the children in Dornach."

But this prophecy did not come to pass. On the contrary. When the reason for Maria's removal from Dornach became known, there was no lack of spitefulness toward the child even from the adults, and especially from the women. Whenever he appeared, he was called a name, about whose meaning he asked in vain at home, and when he spoke to his mother about it, tears welled up in her eyes. She had thought that after the departure from Dornach nothing could hurt her again, and now she found that there were still thorns that could penetrate her heart.

When she had thirsted for contempt, she had not considered the fact that her innocent child would have to share it with her.

She began to court the favor of the vile and the unsympathetic. She provided help and did not allow herself to be deterred by the suspicion and the barely concealed scorn with which her gifts were accepted. When Erich complained about the peasant children, she dismissed it. "They can't help it; you should pity them. No one tells them to be good."

"It would be a waste of time if they did; one has to speak another language with them!" Lisette interrupted, fuming with rage. She would have happily avenged with fire and sword every insult suffered by Maria or the child. She gradually freed herself of all her respect for Count Wolfsberg and fearlessly gave voice to her indignation that he did not come and take care of his daughter and "give those miserable officials and villagers a piece of his mind — with a horse-whip!" she would shout and then pound on the table.

It was incomprehensible to her that Maria refused Wilhelm and his wife's fervent pleas to be allowed to visit, and she never tired of communicating her displeasure about it.

"Believe me," was the answer she finally received, "it would spoil me, weaken me." Maria pressed the palms of her hands to her face and then lifted her head in her old proud manner. "But I must remain strong."

She maintained an unshakable equanimity; she seemed blind and deaf when she encountered defiant expressions or when the mere sight of her elicited insulting whispers.

One day in late autumn, her path led her to an isolated hut whose ancient inhabitant had been freed from all affliction since the countess had been at Wolfsberg. As bent as a bow, she sat on a bench at the door and invited Maria to take a seat next to her. She began by complaining that the articles of clothing she had received from the manor were not quite to her taste, but did conclude with a few words of thanks.

Leaning on her walking stick, she looked up at Maria, who, overcome with repugnance at the ape-like ugliness of the old woman, involuntarily closed her eyes.

"Yes, how you've changed now, to be taking such care of us," she said. "Such a thing never occurred to you when you were living here before." She smiled maliciously. "Well, now, we'll pray your soul free, my daughter and I; you can give the others as much as you like, but they won't pray for you . . . they'll only insult you. But as for what they do themselves, your Ladyship, you'll hear that from me, so that if one of them should dare to say something to your face, you can give it right back to him."

She told her story. She delivered up the secrets of the inhabitants of her village. It was a hair-raising tale of the state of their morals, and the old sibyl invented nothing. Her revelations bore the stamp of truth, although it was a truth that kept pace with the darkest and most debauched creations of fantasy.

Maria interrupted the woman's flow of words at its most torrential and rose. "What horrors," she thought. "No, you should not have turned out this way, you poor, wretched creatures! You should not have had to stumble into the swamp in which you are now sinking. Had there been just a few prudent and merciful people among those who have had absolute rule over you for centuries, they would have led you to an appreciation of good. They had the power; why not a sense of justice, selflessness, a loving heart as well?"

As the child of her ancestors, Maria felt herself to be an accessory to this shameful neglect; nevertheless, she was the last one who would be able to compensate for it. She could give, but she could not advise, teach, or improve — she was herself flawed. Leading people to their true salvation requires an unblemished hand.

She hurried away as though she were being pursued and lay awake that night, restless and feverish. The large bedroom she shared with Erich was vaulted like a chapel. In it hung two masterpieces by Benczur,[34] portraits of Hermann and his son. Countess Agathe had had them painted for her daughter-in-law, and they were the first items that Wilhelm had ordered sent from Dornach to his adored cousin. The beloved figures seemed about to step out of their frames; their kind, devoted eyes seemed to seek Maria's and to follow her wherever she went. She sank down on her bed; her entire soul flamed up in the consuming desire that is eternally present and eternally in vain in all those unfortunates who survive their dearest ones. "To hear your voice just once more, to press a kiss upon your lips, just one more time."

Oh, this incessant demand, never fulfilled, never forgotten, this demand for *one* last time!

All was still in the house and outside as well. For once the storm had folded its wings and ceased its wild song. The quiet days of her early, still unconscious happiness ran through Maria's mind. She lost herself in the memory of every hour spent with her husband, her friend.

He had faithfully kept the promise he had made to her on their engagement: to view what she did for him as an act of grace and what he was allowed to do for her as his greatest happiness. And his behavior to her was only the highest degree of what he exhibited toward everyone. She raised her eyes and her hands to his picture and made a silent vow, "The world shall not lose you entirely; your kindness and your patience will live on. I want to earn the right to practice them in your spirit; I want to earn the trust of the suffering and the errant."

That year winter was early and harsh with its short days, its dim light, its ice and snow. Cut off from communication with the outside world for weeks at a time, Maria would always look first for letters from her father when a postal package could finally be delivered to the manor house, and often she looked in vain. Princess Alma, Carla, and Betty wrote lovingly; the Wilhelms repeated their standing request more and more fervently and expressed their desire for a reunion with ever greater warmth. Aunt Dolph sent inappropriately plucky reports about the doings of society, while Wolfsberg's letters touched only on distant topics, as impersonally as possible.

In the evenings, when ice and snowstorms kept Maria imprisoned in the house, she would sit down at the piano and play, and very often Erich would come, push up a chair, climb up on it, and listen with undivided attention. The child seemed to perceive the beauty of the improvisations that welled up from beneath his mother's fingers. His dark, luminous gaze would rest on her with reverent awe and lower itself almost shyly when she looked at him.

Once she stopped suddenly, took him on her lap, and pressed him to her. He stroked and kissed her cheek, wanted to speak, but choked back the question that was on the tip of his tongue.

"What is it? What do you want to say?" said Maria.

"I would like so much . . . so much — " he faltered again and then, after a pause, continued hesitantly, "I know how to get to Dornach, Mother. You can see the way from the bedroom window; Lisette showed me. She said that poor Dornach is all alone, and that it will be alone a long time. Is it far to Dornach, dear Mother?"

She nodded silently. "Yes."

"But I would like to go to Dornach," he began again, becoming more determined. "Hermann will tell me about the lions. Dornach is not as far as the lions."

"Yes, it is!" she cried in a tone of sharp anguish. "Dornach is farthest of all; it is unreachable!"

The following morning, when Lisette, entering her mistress's room, cried out, "How pale you are, how ill you look!" Maria had to admit that she felt tired and unwell.

Lisette said only, "It must be bad if you're saying it yourself," but she put into action something that she had been planning for quite a while, and she confided during the course of the day to the housemaid that she had carried out a "coup" today, a first-rate "coup."

Maria was hurt that the count had stayed away — at least she could put a stop to that. Lisette knew quite well what she had to do to "give him a good scare."

* * *

At the moment Maria had made her confession of guilt, her father had imagined to himself its dreadful consequences. His daughter's name would be exposed to shame; it would never be mentioned again without arousing the memory of a scandal. And he would be dragged into that disgrace; his brilliant position in society would be annihilated.

But just look! While he was preparing to flee the world as an outcast, it sought him out, more respectful than ever. Strangely enough, Maria had won the public's good opinion through the heroic disregard she had shown for it. High society forgave rather than condemned her; in fact, it did more: it admired her. Fashionable ladies declared that Countess Dornach would always be welcome in their homes.

"'Welcome,' indeed!" cried Betty Wonsheim. "I would meet her at the door on my knees."

And how Carla concurred with her! And what inexpressible pity filled Princess Alma's heart and did not dare to speak itself aloud for fear that it would seem to be an understandable sympathy with the guilty woman and with the sin. Fée, who had had a splendid traveling coach built (heaven only knows *where*, heaven only knows *when* one might need it!), could hardly wait to use it. A trip through the countryside with one's own horses, frequent stops along the way, and a marvelous ending: a sudden leap into the arms of her surprised, her dearest, her adored friend — that would have been just the sort of experience little Fée enjoyed.

Maria's harshest judges were in her own family.

"I've done with her entirely," Aunt Dolph said bluntly to Miss Ninnemann.

The companion answered, not without spiritual arrogance, "She will find consolation for that — in heaven, which awaits the great penitent."

"What did you say — heaven? That may be. There's a heaven for the simple-minded. She did something foolish in order to make amends for a mistake; that may be appreciated there."

Miss Ninnemann turned all colors, from crimson to purple. "I am outraged to my very depths — "

"Because of me?" asked Countess Dolph with a superior smile. "Oh, how awful. No, I beg you, not another word. Take pity on me — I know that my sentiments are mere dogs compared to yours."

Although her own judgment of Maria was severe, she sought to mitigate the harshness of her brother's because of the suffering it caused him. "What is it that you hold against her, after all?" she asked once. "That your blood and that of her mother runs in her veins. Now, my dear, I cannot call the use she made of it unreasonable. She married, remember, with a desire for Tessin in her heart, and she — I know her — dismissed every thought of him. But the memories and feelings one denies — for those of your breed, it's like pushing back sand or snow: it piles up and piles up, it becomes a mountain, and then it crashes over your heads at the first opportunity."

"That woman," muttered Wolfsberg, "and — that man!"

Countess Dolph's mouth twisted into an expression of indescribable mockery. "Must I, the old spinster, tell you that the crown of love, unlike that of the Macedonians, is not reserved for 'the most worthy'? It would be a boring world if only paragons of virtue were to make conquests. I beg you, stop tormenting yourself. You cannot be angry forever, and a grievance that one must abandon eventually should be given up as soon as possible."

113

Time passed. The first days of spring arrived. The communication between father and daughter was still limited to a sporadic correspondence.

Then Countess Dolph appeared one morning in her brother's study. Her left eye was contracted and blinked dully. She had gone driving around the city with her March rheumatism, the worst of all, and had just come from a farewell visit to the Wonsheims. All was not well with them. On the urgent advice of their physicians, the two couples were setting off on a long journey. Clemens needed distraction at all costs. Ever since the terrible misfortune he had caused by thoughtlessly goading a child's ambition into taking a fatal risk, the wretched man had been in serious danger of succumbing to melancholy.

"He, of course, does not intend to show himself to Maria, but the two women want very much to bid her farewell. Do you think that would be all right?" the countess asked.

"I don't know," he answered.

"She is rather unwell."

"Who?"

"Why, Maria."

"Has she written?"

"Not she. Lisette, the old panicmonger, sent a letter behind her back to Dr. Hofer, and he departed immediately for Wolfsberg."

The count sat at his desk, held a pen in his hand, and tapped its point vigorously on an already finished document. "What a lot of overreactions!"

"He did not stay long; he was already here with me today in a rage about the country's terrible public transportation." She moved closer to the fireplace where a wood-fire was burning. "Three patients had held off dying till he returned; as soon as they've been dispatched, he will be here to see you."

"He should have come right away," Wolfsberg responded impatiently. "Why am I the last to hear of all this?"

"So that you don't worry unnecessarily . . . quite unnecessarily! It isn't serious at all." She had forgotten, had wanted to forget, half of what the doctor had said, and she withheld most of the other half from her brother. Her pains had become almost intolerable. "Good-bye for now," she said, "I must rest *anticipando*; I have company this evening, the entire menagerie, as Madame de — de — what was her name? said; well, that woman in the eighteenth century, when Paris was still the peak of culture and was the coffeehouse of Europe, Madame — I've forgotten what her name was; my memory is failing. Yet another of the many signs of approaching senility. Yes, my dear fellow, hold on to your descendants; one's contemporaries die off. From one day to the next, you could be a brother without a sister."

She thought it fitting to say that, but would have been quite astonished had anyone believed her.

When she was gone, Wolfsberg drove to the ministry, presided over a meeting, received visitors — just as always. And at the same time he had the

114

constant sensation that he was choking. Toward evening he came home, began restlessly pacing up and down in his rooms, and listened for every ring of the doorbell. A difficult, wearying hour crept by. Finally the door was flung open for the doctor.

He was a man in his fifties, stocky and powerful, with a respectable bald spot, but with hair that was still dark. The frank expression on his handsome, smooth-shaven face and his straightforward demeanor won the confidence of others at first sight, a confidence that he had never failed to justify.

The count went to meet him and extended both hands to him. "Dear Professor, faithful friend — you were there — thank you."

"No thanks necessary," Hofer answered dryly. His small brown eyes fixed on Wolfsberg, he continued in the colloquial tone he often used. "It was my damned duty to look after her, and, if you'll excuse me, it's yours too. You and I, we've known her the same length of time, and we should know that the woman deserves some consideration."

Wolfsberg wiped his brow. "A lot has changed, friend. Let's get to the point! How is she?" He leaned back against the window; the doctor stood before him.

"A strange question," he said. "Strange that even for you the old rule holds true: 'The family is always the last to know.' Ahem! The woman's had to endure too much. You know something, Count? Stop sulking right now; otherwise you may regret it," and he clapped him on the shoulder.

"Doctor, Professor . . . regret . . . you see things too darkly . . . your only fault."

"I see only what you will see too. Go there tomorrow; put a little order back into your knight's castle, but don't stay long, and don't go there again too soon. Even your visits will agitate the invalid — "

"The invalid?"

" — and all excitement, no matter how trivial, may have the worst consequences for her. It is quite a good thing to let her doze the days away and to limit herself to her child's company. If she doesn't overtax her strength, it may be possible to take her south in the fall. But," he raised his forefinger threateningly, "she must be conscious that no one bears her a grudge of any sort. She deserves admiration. Anyone who hurts that woman is committing a mortal sin, I tell you."

Half an hour later the count informed his sister that he would be traveling with the night train to Wolfsberg and had his bags packed. The meal that was served to him in his room was left untouched. He wrote a few lines to his office and threw the answer on the table unread. Leaning back in an armchair, he stared into space. She had knelt here on this spot, her head on his heart . . . . Suddenly, involuntarily, his hands folded. The man, to whom faith was nothing but a bridle[35] for the masses and a necessary solace for the world's disinherited, prayed now to the God of love and mercy, of whom he had not thought in years. "Spare her for me," he cried out to Him. That was all he knew how to say in his torment — the beginning and the end of his eloquence. "Almighty God, spare her for me!"

The next day he arrived at Wolfsberg before the telegram that was to announce his visit. The surprise of the servants, the exclamations of Lisette, who had just stepped into the courtyard as he drove up, apprised him of that.

"The count! Isn't that something!" cried the old woman, acted very astonished, and answered his enquiry about Maria with a few hastily spoken words, "By the pine trees . . . in the garden . . . I must ask you . . . I want to prepare her . . . ."

He did not listen. While all was in confusion at the manor and in the offices and sworn enemies were uniting in their shared annoyance at his arrival, he walked quickly toward the large group of trees at the southern end of the garden. How everything had run wild! The paths were grown over with grass, the meadows had been consumed by weeds, the shrubbery was untrimmed; its bare, weak stems had grown high. There were innumerable open spaces instead of the formerly shady avenues. From a distance he could already see his daughter. She sat on a mossy bench under the mighty trees — transparently pale, thin in her close-fitting black dress — and watched the child, who was busily constructing a small grotto. Her father was already quite close when she heard his steps crackling on the path, which was thickly strewn with fallen pine needles. She raised her head.

"Maria!" he cried, and tears came to his eyes.

She stood up, wanted to speak, to rush to him, but sank back mutely, with a smile of boundless gratitude.

He bent down to her and pressed a long kiss upon her forehead. She whispered something unintelligible. Her nostrils quivered; her lips were parted; she inhaled audibly.

Wolfsberg sat down next to her. "If only I had known," he said. "Why not write and tell me . . . how unfair." Overcome with emotion, he drew her hands to his mouth and kissed them and said quietly, "No one loves you the way I do, and no one has hurt you so much."

Everything was a reproach to him: her careworn appearance, her neglected surroundings, the aloofness of the child, who had stopped his game and was looking at him gravely and questioningly without greeting him.

Suddenly the little boy's eyes sparkled happily. He approached his mother. "Look there," he said, placed the palm of his small hand on her cheek, and forced her to turn her head. The sun was going down; its last horizontal rays shimmered between the trunks of the trees, and the face of the child glowed in the reflection. Golden light played on his dark, wavy hair.

Wolfsberg looked at him with painful admiration. "Well, what is the matter with you?" he began. "You're not even looking at me. Don't you recognize me anymore?"

"Oh, yes — oh, yes!" Erich answered, bowed his head, and turned all his attention to a beetle attempting to climb up a blade of grass.

Maria, too, did not dare to look up. The memory of the loathing with which Countess Agathe had pushed the child away flashed through her, and she murmured, "Forgive him; he has become so shy in our solitude."

"We'll win his confidence, never fear," said her father and held out his right hand to the little boy. "Shake hands, little Wolfsberg, shake hands, my grandson. To our friendship!"

The count remained at home for some time, and all those in his service discovered how justified their dismay at his arrival had been. He took them to task; his most shameless exploiters, his most arrogant officials broke out in a cold sweat when he, with clenched teeth and without raising his voice, said, "You will live to regret it if on my return I do not find every sign of negligence corrected and more."

He postponed his departure from one day to the next. He had grown fond of Erich; he concerned himself more with him than he had with Maria when she was at that tender age. He was not given to half-measures. He wanted the grandson he had acknowledged to be acknowledged by all the world and to be raised for a brilliant future. When he expounded upon his ambitious plans to Maria, however, he met with resistance. She wanted the reverse for Erich, the reverse of all that seemed desirable to her father; in fact, she demanded his solemn promise that she would retain the right to determine the child's future as long as she lived as well as after her death.

He looked at her, appalled and hesitant, but he was no longer able to give an answer other than "Yes" to any desire she expressed.

Her unshakable composure moved him to the depths of his soul. It seemed to him to be the composure of someone who has half departed this world, who no longer hopes or desires. In the last year of her life, her mother, in her tranquil moments, had worn the same expression of quiet despair. Maria's resemblance to that unhappy woman was now complete, and Wolfsberg shuddered sometimes when he encountered her unexpectedly.

On the evening before his departure they had gone from the drawing room, where they had taken their tea, into the adjoining alcove. From its high, narrow windows, one could see over the trees in the garden, past the village, into a pasture partially covered with rubble that had rolled down from the quarry. Twilight had fallen, and, in its deceptive shimmer, one seemed to be looking at an immense graveyard. Wolfsberg, deep in thought, looked out the window. One last time he attempted to persuade Maria to exchange her gloomy residence for a home on one of his estates in the Tyrol or in Upper Austria. "There it would be easier for me to reach you, and Aunt Dolph, for whom the journey here is too arduous, would be able to visit you as well. And the others, the many others, who love you. All the messages that little Fée sent with me! If you absolutely won't permit her to visit you, she has threatened to come without your permission."

"Do not allow it!" Maria implored. Her cheeks were tinged a deep red. "Dear Father, I cannot see anyone. Let me bury myself here, let me be dead for everyone; it's the only way I can bear to be alive."

At Wolfsberg's departure, his employees, along with what were not always their "better halves," assembled in the castle courtyard. The head of the village was there as well. The count had relieved the villagers of part of their debts, against his own convictions but at Maria's intercession. He came down the steps with Maria and Erich, responded with a dismissive gesture to the submissive bows and curtsies of those who were awaiting him, embraced his daughter, kissed and blessed his grandson, and leapt into the carriage.

Maria remained motionless, looking after him. Suddenly she noticed that the others had not moved from the spot either, but were waiting, with deferential demeanor, for her to dismiss them. Their insolent hostility had been transformed into a servile one.

*   *   *

A year after Hermann's death, Tessin wrote to Maria. He would be transferred to another, higher position, also abroad, later in the year; before taking up that post he would come back home for a time. In stirring sentences that breathed deep, unchanging love, he begged her to grant him a reunion and connected his request to a hope that was perhaps too audacious to be fulfilled. But, he wrote, he lived for it, and to be forced to relinquish it would mean his ruin.

Maria read with horror and alarm. So the past was not buried after all? The hand of the originator of her unatoneable sin reached out for her still? The hour of her degradation rose up before her mind's eye — incomprehensible, a hellish mystery . . . . Her heart stood still; her teeth chattered. Summoning all her strength, she went to the desk and hurriedly wrote a few lines to her father. "Answer for me — you know all . . . . Help me. Save me from this man. Protect me from the danger of ever hearing from him again."

She enclosed Tessin's letter with her own and urged a messenger on horseback to bring it to the post office with the utmost speed.

In her thoughts she accompanied her messenger. By now he could be at the quarry and by now at the bridge, and if he really galloped, he would yet arrive before the departure of the mail cart. And that cart would take four hours to reach the railway station. Four full hours . . . if they were only over, she would breathe easier.

"Now," she thought as the castle clock struck ten, "the letter is on the train."

She had sent the servants to bed and now paced restlessly up and down in her bedroom, until, utterly exhausted, she at last sank down on her bed, which was next to Erich's little one. He slept soundly and looked intelligent and sweet.

His mother gathered strength and courage from the sight of him; her worries suddenly seemed foolish to her. What difference did it make if the answer to that letter, which had flown at her like an arrow shot from behind a tree, came a day earlier or a day later? What difference did it make? She exhorted herself to be reasonable; she reproached her will for its weakness, because it could not prevail over the activity of her agitated nerves, over the wild beating of her heart. Toward morning she fell into a light sleep, disturbed by confused dreams, and woke up bathed in a cold sweat. She rose with difficulty and sent Erich into the garden with his nurse. Toward noon he came for his lesson as usual into the alcove, where Maria was waiting for him.

"Mother," he cried, "someone has come, a gentleman, with the postmaster's white horses, and one of them is limping."

She had leapt up, had cast a quick glance toward the door, as though she wanted to flee, and then had sunk back into her chair. "Someone has come," she repeated. "Do you know who?"

No, he did not know.

But she knew . . . . Tessin had not waited for her answer — he had come.

The door that led from the corridor into the adjoining room was flung open. One heard Lisette's shrill exclamation, "For heaven's sake!" "I have orders not to admit anyone," a servant said loudly.

"Mother," cried Erich, "why are they shouting so?" He spread his arms out and placed himself protectively in front of her. "Don't be afraid!"

And now Lisette burst in, quite agitated. "Just think — he calls himself Count Tessin, and I could swear it's the same . . . . But what's the matter with you?"

Maria had risen; her face had assumed an unusual expression. Grimly and coldly, she looked at Tessin, who had just entered and who turned deathly pale at the sight of her.

Erich plunged toward him. "Go away, you, go away. We don't want you — " and he raised his fist threateningly.

Tessin's mouth twisted; he smiled at the child with a mixture of embarrassment and mockery. He wished himself far away from here; he cursed his own impatience.

In the memory he had lovingly cherished, he had always pictured Maria just as she had been in the sweetest and most victorious hour of his life. In his thoughts he had held this most beautiful woman in his arms thousands upon thousands of times. The mad desire for her that had often seized him while abroad had grown from minute to minute ever since he had stepped onto his native soil. He had no doubt — she loved him still; she had always loved only him; she awaited him with the same yearning with which he had hurried toward her —

119

And now he was here; he had reached his goal, and what it offered him was a cruel disappointment, which he lacked the composure to conceal. Slowly he approached and bowed silently.

Maria waved to Lisette to take the boy away. He resisted but had to obey. At the door he turned around and cast a look full of defiance and distrust at Tessin.

XXI.

Maria watched the child leave. Sparks glittered before her eyes. It seemed to her as though the wall she leaned against was swaying, as though the small round windowpanes were spinning like tops, bursting like soap bubbles. She bit her lips. She wanted to remain steadfast; she wanted to exert mastery over her waning senses. Once again her memory recalled for her the magic words of old: "Stay calm!"

"How dare you?" she uttered suddenly. "What do you want? Why didn't you wait for my answer?"

"What a question . . . ." he replied, disconcerted by this reception. "Because of my impatience, my longing — "

"For what awaits you here?"

"What awaits me here? You mean the pain of finding you ailing." " — and dreadfully changed," he added mentally.

The most conflicting feelings were at war within him: pity, resentment, defiance, and melancholy. Every advantage seemed within his reach, every happiness. Should he now seek his happiness with a faded woman at his side? But — it was *she*! She who had inspired in him the most fervent passion of his life . . . . He felt anew her captivating influence and abandoned himself to it. The consciousness of an outrage committed against this poor woman awakened within him, and at the same time — only liars maintained that he was incapable of generous impulses — the resolution to make amends for his guilt.

He had remained standing, his hat in his hand, and now took a seat, uninvited, across from Maria. Gradually he rediscovered in that pale countenance the features that had been so dear to him. It bore the traces of great inner anguish, which had been suffered for his sake — no slight gratification for his vanity.

Tessin spoke a few words of sympathy and regret; to himself, however, he said, "She is young; she will recover; she will bloom again in my arms. I want to be the god who breathes color back into her cheeks, who brings a smile to her lips, who awakens her from the dead and leads her back to all the joys of life."

He began by declaring his unchanged love for her. He told her about the ingenuity he had exhibited in keeping himself informed of everything that concerned her. He therefore knew about her "noble gesture of renunciation" as well and vowed that he would make good the claim it made upon him.

With a sort of dull surrender, Maria endured his presence, the gaze he directed unswervingly at her. Her own remained so absent, so empty, that Tessin could not ward off a moment of doubt as to the ready feasibility of his divine mission. In an irritated, involuntarily challenging tone, he concluded, "You deprived your son of the name that was due him by law; that can only have been done with the intention of giving him the name that in fact belongs to him: mine."

Now she made a vigorous defensive motion. "Give him your name and thereby give you a right to the child — you?" She leaned forward. In her eyes a flame of contempt had ignited. It struck him like a burning arrow.

He winced, struggled for self-control, and nevertheless cried out, beside himself, "Countess . . . Maria, you loved me!"

She bowed her head; her cheeks flushed a fiery red. "I thought that I loved you, and you — were clever, you knew how to kindle a sense of guilt toward you in me. Then you enlisted an accomplice, and with his treacherous help you came and took me by surprise, baser, more dishonorable than a thief, and I threw myself away on you . . . . And after the irrevocable had happened, after the sin had been committed — a sin that can no more be washed away by tears of remorse than a cliff by the waves that break at its base — then the man at whose side I had until then been blind became dearer to me day by day. He taught me about the love that is eternal; he, in whose soul the purest goodness and fidelity were united . . . . And such a sensation, in a heart that had become unworthy of his . . . . The rarest, most precious happiness squandered — at such a price!" A shudder of revulsion ran through her.

Inwardly filled with indignation, though outwardly stiff and impassive, Tessin had listened to her. How he hated her now, the fool, who — just a little too late — had fallen in love with her husband; how ridiculous he found her, with her sentimentality and her morbid remorse. A little cooling off was necessary, so he murmured mockingly, "How you must have cursed me."

"Only myself . . . . You lack a sense of justice; I had one and nevertheless betrayed the noblest trust, practiced deception — for you!"

Her gaze glided over him, and he experienced it as something physical that wiped away all value, all self-assurance, all the imagined glory . . . . He gnashed his teeth; he felt he needed to defend himself by any means necessary.

"You are becoming agitated," he said icily. "Do you want to kill yourself?"

"No, I want to live in order to raise my child . . . . I want to teach him to be upright and true and strong, an enemy of all that glitters and pretends and lies . . . . He shall — " her labored breathing faltered.

"Just say it bluntly," cried Tessin with a bitter smile. "He shall become the opposite of all that you consider me to be. Good luck, Countess — may your childrearing succeed. But I would advise you not to be too harsh — many a lesson fails to take effect precisely because it was administered too ruthlessly."

Maria had lowered her head, was staring vacantly, and, preoccupied, only nodded at his words. "He shall also," she began, "never learn that you are his . . . his — " it was impossible for her to say it. "You will always remain a stranger to him! I demand that, I will stand guard, and it must remain that way when I am no longer here to protect him from your influence, from your example. A stranger. Swear it to me — or no — promise me . . . . But not the way that men like you promise a woman something, you who think that to treat a woman dishonorably does not dishonor you. Why? Why? Perhaps because she cannot call your type to account." She trembled and shivered, and it appeared that he felt a certain satisfaction at her extreme agitation. He was the essence of composed, cold-blooded superiority; he was strong and healthy; he had nerves of steel.

"Countess," he said in a warning tone, "you want something from me and yet insult me incessantly. Is that wise?"

Maria pressed both hands to her forehead. "Unwise!" she moaned, "altogether foolish and unwise . . . . Forgive me . . . ." It sounded shrill, like a cry wrung with overwhelming force from her innermost being, from her resistant will. "Forgive me and grant my request."

He pretended to think about it and said after a while, "It shall be done."

Maria added quickly, "By all that is — but what is holy to you?" she concluded, disheartened.

Now his expression became solemn and firm. "The memory of the hour that you would like to expunge from your life and that I would not exchange for all the riches on earth. By that memory I promise it." He stood up slowly. A wild desire to pull her to him, to press her to his breast once again, overcame him.

Then Maria rose too, and they stood face to face.

Later, after he had achieved everything for which he had striven, when fortune followed him wherever he went, when any undertaking seemed inevitably to lead to success, he sometimes thought of that short, strange, silent battle between himself and a frail dying woman — in which he was defeated.

She had pointed to the door, and he had restrained himself and obeyed.

Maria remained standing . . . she had to remain standing. If she were to betray herself now, she herself, what folly that would be! No, she does not do it, she will not, she is strong.

The door opens again; Erich comes running in. "Mother!" he cries, "The man has already left."

"Yes . . . yes, indeed."

And now Lisette, who has followed the child in, says, "Strange, how strange! Felix Tessin — I don't recognize the name, but the man . . . . What could he have wanted? I could swear that he is the same man who was the last to be seen with poor Wolfi."

"That may be so — " Maria stammered, indistinctly. "Brother and sister murdered, thanks to him — " and she fell to the ground in a faint.

A long time passed before she regained consciousness. In a panic, Lisette had had telegrams sent to the professor, to Wolfsberg, to Wilhelm: "Countess ill. Come immediately." Half out of her wits, she tore at her hair and could not stop screaming, "She is dead. My child is dead!" However, when the first quiver ran through the body of the unconscious woman, when her eyes opened for the first time, Lisette's despair made way for the most unshakable conviction and optimism.

With difficulty, Maria spoke a few words: "Have Wilhelm and Helmi come, right away, do you hear? Right away!" A crushing fear seemed to be oppressing her; she asked for the child, and when he was brought to her she did not recognize him and thought that he was little Hermann. "There you are — " she murmured, "that was a deep sleep . . . . Oh, how I've longed for my firstborn!"

Night fell; the invalid lay motionless. A bucket of ice was placed next to her bed. Lisette and Klara took turns freshening the compresses on her forehead.

"She does not see us, you may be sure of that, Miss," whispered the maid. "Oh, God, and her eyes! Like blue flames, covered by veils."

On the table stood a covered lamp; the weak halo it cast upon the ceiling captured Maria's gaze. Billowing waves formed in its pale shimmer, and a white swan floated on them, and lovely music resounded in the air above. It suddenly stopped; a star had fallen from the heavens and the star was a woman and horrible monsters tore her to pieces. Hundreds of grimacing faces, heads without bodies, floated toward her, eyes without heads, so many eyes, which bored into hers. She was not afraid; it all seemed natural to her. Natural, too, that she was lying on her bed and at the same time was standing up there, in the flickering light, at Hermann's side. He pointed to her and said, "I see your heart; it is bleeding, and it has a black spot, a small, small spot that darkens the world."

Outside the storm howled, whistled around the house, flung torrents of rain against the windowpanes, rattled the hinges of the doors, and threw itself against the gate, which resisted it, moaning.

Lisette said, "That confounded weather! It's keeping you awake, my poor child!"

"In Dornach it is calm," Maria answered and, after a pause, "Do you believe — do you believe it, dear old Lisette?"

"Do I believe what? What would you like me to believe?"

"That they will allow me to lie in the crypt there?"

"What nonsense you're talking!"

"Dust with dust, but — how wonderful . . . ." She made an attempt to turn herself. "One of them has come — "

"Who? I don't understand you."

"But you brought him yourself," she responded in a low voice with a hint of impatience. "His father sent him. He is to lead me to Dornach, to my beloved Dornach — " she smiled joyously as she spoke the name, " — to my Hermann, there, where he is now . . . . We will lie hand in hand behind the stones. Not a single sound will reach us, not a single voice — not even the voice of conscience."

123

"She's delirious, and I tell you, the priest must be sent for," Klara whispered to Lisette. The latter responded sharply.

"Ha! Delirious, is she? She wouldn't dream of it. She's talking in her sleep; she's done that since she was a child."

Maria sank into a dull half-sleep, from which she would wake up with a start now and then to call for Wilhelm and Helmi. Toward morning she became quieter, and the district doctor, who had been called, found her in this state. When he heard that Professor Hofer was expected at any time, he expressed the desire to meet the famous doctor and resolved to return later. He kept his opinion about the invalid's condition to himself, and he found it superfluous to prescribe anything.

Lisette was triumphant. Didn't the doctor's behavior prove she was right? Would he have gone away without saying anything, without even writing a prescription, if he had had the least apprehension?

She found it very fortunate that a telegram in response to hers arrived that hour from the professor's home, saying that he was away for three days. She therefore had time to cancel her summons, and he would not need to scold her again as "the old scaredy-cat."

Lisette's optimism was contagious. High spirits reigned in the entire castle. The castle steward resumed his siskin's interrupted singing lessons and whistled to him unremittingly, one verse at a time, the song "When I rise early in the morning." The men walked with a firm step once more; the women slammed the doors noisily. Everything returned to the old patterns.

Maria had herself carried to the sofa and had the sofa moved to the window. She was exhausted and almost dazed, and she imagined constantly that she had heard the carriage that was bringing Wilhelm and Helmi rolling into the courtyard.

"Now, be reasonable," Lisette exhorted. "They can't be here yet, despite the relay horses that the steward sent, unless a miracle has happened, or — unless they took a special train."

One of these contingencies must have taken place, because toward evening the people Maria had longed for were there, accompanied by Dr. Weise. With cheerful expressions, the servants ran to meet them and announced that she was doing better, she was doing well.

Lisette rushed down the steps; she almost threw herself on her knees before the couple and almost threw her arms around the doctor. "May God reward the lady and the gentlemen for coming so quickly . . . now she will be happy." Continually urging them forward, she guided them up the stairs and through the corridors.

"You go first," said Wilhelm to the doctor, "and decide whether the countess may see us."

He disregarded Lisette's objections; she had to consent to announcing Weise, who was admitted immediately, while Wilhelm and Helmi waited in the next room. He, quite agitated; she, anxious, bent, with pale cheeks. The comforting assurances with which they had been received inspired them with little confidence. They trembled when Lisette appeared at last.

"Come in, come in! She is asking for you, and for no one but you," she cried and discreetly withdrew.

"Well, then, in God's name," said Wilhelm, and Helmi laid her hand gently on the doorknob. Just then Weise came out of the room.

"Nothing can be done," he whispered, deeply grieved. "A rupture of the heart, about which, of course, one should not imagine — well, in a word, it's over."

Wilhelm staggered, as though someone had struck him.

"But — she is still alive . . . ."

"Still, yes, still," and Weise pushed open the door.

Maria lay stretched out straight. The last light of day cast its pale glow over her features, already transfigured by the noble majesty of death. Encircled by the golden splendor of her hair, her head rested on the pillows, and she made a futile effort to lift it as Wilhelm and Helmi entered. The latter stroked the hand of the invalid with trembling fingers.

"Thank you — for coming . . . thank you . . . and a request — " said Maria. "You see that I shall not be permitted to live for the child . . . nor will I be permitted to expiate any part of my sin . . . ."

"You have atoned for it, oh, God in heaven, how you have atoned!" cried Helmi.

"Repented, but not atoned — I could never have done that . . . . The awareness of that makes life difficult . . . and death, too . . . ."

Wilhelm began in a low voice, and then, like a shout, it burst from his breast, "No, no, you will not die!"

"Yes, I will — and *you*, good parents, *you* have one more son — mine . . . . Yes?"

Both were sobbing. "Yes."

Helmi pushed up the pillows in order to raise the sick woman's head a little, and Maria's gaze rested on her with an expression that seemed to come from another world.

And now, out of the deep silence, a carriage was heard approaching. The beating of hooves and the crack of a whip resounded before the gate, which was pushed back along its iron track, and a heavy conveyance rumbled in.

Maria had listened attentively. "Father . . . my poor father," she said. Fear and apprehension were reflected in her dying face; an anxious pleading was in her voice. "Wilhelm, Helmi — in my desk — a letter to you — contains my will . . . protect the child from every other influence — from *every* other influence . . . . Swear it — "

"Rest assured," said Wilhelm, and now his tone was steady and firm, "we, and we alone, will assume responsibility for this soul."

"My poor father!" Maria repeated. "Happiness is not where he seeks it. To be good is happiness — simple, selfless, and good, like Hermann, like both of you . . . . Erich will someday continue the work I have begun in my Hermann's spirit here in Wolfsberg . . . the work I was interrupted in . . . he will . . . . Where is Erich?" she asked, in a louder voice.

A merry laugh rang out. "He is coming, and who else?" said someone, crossing the threshold — and Fée came floating into the room, holding Erich by the hand. "Here she is, here is your little Fée; now throw her out, if you can bring yourself to do it." She had approached the sofa, started back suddenly, and moaned, "Oh! Oh!"

Maria looked at her, and a faint smile strayed around her mouth and greeted this emissary of the living who had made her way into the room, so lovely, so fresh and rosy, whose laughter was like the song of a lark.

Seized by a cowardly impulse, Fée wanted to flee, but she controlled herself. She stayed, lifted Erich up to his mother, gently and tenderly took Maria's arm, laid it around the child's neck, and stammered, "You called him."

"Little Fée," said Maria, "farewell, dear little Fée."

Now the young woman lost her composure completely. She threw herself impetuously on Maria's breast and broke into a storm of tears and lamentations. Wilhelm freed the dying woman from her grasp; he wanted to lead Fée out, but she pulled herself away and sank down onto a cushion at the end of the room, where she writhed in convulsive efforts to suppress her sobs.

Lisette came to get Erich and received her mistress's thanks "for many years of constant loyalty." "You, too, are commended to these noble people — they will not separate you from the child. Don't love him too much — not the way you loved your grown-up child, poor old Lisette."

"I will never love anyone else so much," and with burning, trembling lips she kissed the precious hand of her one and only darling. Her every nerve twitched convulsively; she could not endure it. She took Erich, who, mute and distressed, hardly dared to breathe, and carried him away.

Helmi had knelt down before her. "Maria, dearest, beloved Maria," she implored in a low voice, "do not depart this life unreconciled with God; fulfill your duty as a Christian . . . prepare yourself to lay your head on the heart of the All-bountiful."

"The — All-bountiful?"

"In whom you believe — "

"In whom I believe?" Longingly she repeated Helmi's words in a whisper. "All is lost, Helmi — the belief in providence . . . even the belief in my free will . . . and yet I still have only one wish . . . ." Her last strength exhausted itself in the words, "Oh, if only I had never done wrong!"

*　　*　　*

The telegram that had been sent to Wolfsberg was forwarded to him at Countess Dolph's estate, where he had appeared for a short visit. It found him there late in the evening. He departed immediately. An express train brought him to the first station of the local railway that would take him further. Now began the agony of waiting, from one slow train to the next, of limping along behind a creeping locomotive. Wolfsberg was tempted to jump out and run alongside the train in order at least to have the feeling that he was making progress. Then a thought seized him once again, as though an iron clamp were gripping his chest — "Why such haste? What are you hurrying toward?" He was certain that a sorrow awaited him that was beyond what he could bear. Tortured by fear and impatience, he arrived by means of a wretched conveyance at the last post station before Wolfsberg. There he could be provided with only a worn-out nag. He swung himself into the saddle, furiously urged the horse forward, and took out his angry despair on the unfortunate animal.

It was growing dark when he arrived at the village. He was met by the monotonous ringing of the death knell. People stood together in groups; a whole procession walked along the lane toward the manor. One more blow with his cane on the flank of the exhausted, wheezing horse; it leapt forward, fell, jumped up, and the next moment broke down entirely. The rider extricated himself from the stirrups. A stabbing pain in his foot slowed his gait, and he struggled along behind the procession. Four lights swung at its head, surrounded by whitish clouds of smoke. Wolfsberg suppressed his pain, strained forward with grim effort, and cried, "Stop! Stop! Someone come and help me!"

His voice went unheard by the pilgrims murmuring their prayers. At the gate to the grounds the lamps had been lit. The priest in his vestments, the sextons, and the choirboys with lanterns and censers passed into the courtyard.

"Wait! Help me!" Wolfsberg gasped, half-dead with anxiety.

This time he was heard. The procession halted, and the people looked around; for a long time they could not distinguish anything in the darkness, until suddenly a boy said, "It's the count; he's standing there by the milestone. Something has happened to him."

One person whispered it to the next — but no one did anything more.

At last an old, crippled man took pity on him, went to him, supported him, and led him to the castle.

Almost at the same time as the priest, Wolfsberg entered the death chamber. The windows were wide open. A dark cloud hung in the sky; it resembled a huge bird with widespread wings. The moon it veiled cast an abundance of silvery light onto a spot on the horizon. Maria's eyes, already dimmed, rested on that spot. There, where it was bright, where the transfiguring glow radiated outward — lay Dornach.

Notes

[1] The "one-year volunteers" were young men from the educated classes who, in return for agreeing to feed, clothe, and equip themselves during their military service, were released into the army reserve after only one year of service in the standing army.

[2] Bertrand de Born (ca.1140–ca.1215), Vicomte d'Hautefort, was a trouble-making troubadour who believed in battle for the sake of battle. Dolph's reference is to the second verse of a poem by Uhland, "Bertran de Born": "Is this the man who boasts / And brags so insolently: / That he never requires more / Than half his wit?" (my translation).

[3] Julius Blüthner (1824–1910) founded a piano factory in 1854 in Leipzig; its grand pianos were famous worldwide.

[4] In this description of Tessin, Wolfsberg presumably refers to Friedrich Nietzsche's *Beyond Good and Evil* (1886); one of the premises of this text is that adherence to conventional morality is part of an inferior mentality. "Manfred-like good looks" is a reference to Byron's dramatic poem, "Manfred" (1816). The tortured protagonist describes his lost love as follows: "Her faults were mine — her virtues were her own — / I loved her, and destroy'd her! . . . Not with my hand, but heart — which broke her heart — / It gazed on mine, and withered."

[5] The young, unmarried daughters of a count are called a Germanized version (*Komtessen*) of the French word *comtesses*; older, married women of the family are called countesses (*Gräfinnen*). Ebner wrote two well-known novellas about this category of Austrian girlhood, *Komtesse Muschi* and *Komtesse Paula*, which were published together as *Zwei Komtessen* in 1885. These have been translated into English and appear in *Seven Stories by Marie von Ebner-Eschenbach*, trans. and ed. Helga H. Harriman, Columbia, SC: Camden House, 1986.

[6] The literal translation would be "Dornach Valley."

[7] Pierre Nepveu was a fifteenth-century French sculptor and master of masonry.

[8] French: "Hoping for better"; Antoine Latour (1808–1881) was a French writer.

[9] Jean Petitot (1607–1691) was a Swiss painter of enamel miniatures of well-known pictures.

[10] The literal translation is "play St. Aloysius." St. Aloysius (1568–1591) is the patron saint of youth. His religious convictions became evident when he was seven; at an early age he took a vow of chastity and eventually joined the Jesuits.

[11] Alexander Emanuel Köchert (1825–1879) was a Viennese jeweler; in addition to having a shop in Vienna, he was jeweler to the court of the Austrian emperor.

[12] The Marquise du Deffand (1697–1780) married at twenty-one. She soon separated from her husband and then led a very free life. She had a famous Paris salon, which was visited by Voltaire and Montesquieu, among others. Eventually her lady companion left her employ and took most of the marquise's salon guests with her. Du Deffand is also famous for her correspondence with Horace Walpole (1717–1797), an English politician and writer from an aristocratic family. They met in 1765 in Paris and corresponded un-

til her death. Her letters to him were published in 1810; his letters to various correspondents have also been published. He has been called the best letter-writer in the English language.

[13] *Begum Somru* was a play written by Friedrich Halm. It was performed at the Hofburgtheater in Vienna in 1867–68. The character Arthur Dyce is the unfaithful lover of the female protagonist Begum. (Burkhard Bittrich, ed., *Unsühnbar*, by Marie von Ebner-Eschenbach, Kritische Texte und Deutungen, no. 1 [Bonn: Bouvier, 1978], 311.)

The Stuwer family were famous pyrotechnists in Vienna for a century; the founding father did his first firework show in the Prater in 1774.

[14] Latin: "The base of the heart — the apex of the heart."

[15] Bittrich (280) notes that although the seventh through ninth editions of the novel have "Turkish" rather than "malicious" (*"tückisch"*) as the adjective modifying tobacco, this word is most probably a typographical error that happened to be mistakenly retained in these later editions, since earlier versions use the more appropriate "malicious."

[16] The Girondists were a political party during the period of the French Revolution (1791–1793). Although they were primarily representatives of the liberal bourgeoisie, they helped to overthrow the monarchy. Anarchy followed, which they were powerless to arrest, and other political groups were able to turn the masses against them. Twenty-one members were executed by guillotine.

[17] French: "Let's go! Let's go!"

[18] Moritz von Schwind (1804–1871) was an Austrian painter. His painting cycle "Die schöne Melusine" (1869–70) hangs in Vienna.

[19] The vaulting surcingle is a leather band that goes around the horse's rib cage, behind the withers. It is traditionally used in lunging (see note 35) with beginning riders to help them establish a good "seat"; using it for general riding, jumping, and hunting would be very challenging.

[20] August the Strong (1670–1733) became King of Poland and Elector of Saxony. He had magnificent buildings erected in Dresden and Warsaw, which were home to his courts, and held court in the manner of Louis XIV.

[21] The *minuet à la reine* is an eighteenth-century French court dance.

[22] Christoph Jamnitzer (1563–1618) and his grandfather Wenzel Jamnitzer (1508–1585) were the most talented members of a Nuremberg family of goldsmiths. Among other things, they made elaborate pitchers, bowls, and centerpieces.

Anton Eisenhoit (1553–1603) was a silversmith and copperplate engraver whose work combined gothic elements with renaissance forms.

Johann Melchior Dinglinger (1664–1731) was a goldsmith; after 1698 he was the court goldsmith of August the Strong. His work belongs to the best of the baroque period. The seventh, eighth, and ninth editions of Ebner's novel have the incorrect spelling "Dillinger" (Bittrich 280).

[23] This reference is to Heinrich Wilhelm Döbel (1699–1759), a forester's son who became a huntsman in the service of various princes, one of whom was the Duke of Brunswick

in Blankenburg. He wrote a three-volume work on hunting that was published in 1746 and includes, in the section on the *Fuchsprellen*, a complete description of a procession he once observed; Ebner's procession scene as well as elements of the dinner scene after the battue are taken from Döbel's account. A *Fuchsprellen* (translated in the text as "fox hunt") is an activity in which foxes and other small animals are released from cages and onto sheets stretched tight. Two "hunters" pick up opposite ends of these sheets and toss the animals up in the air until the animals either die or, now dazed, can be clubbed to death.

[24] Italian: "All right; very well."

[25] French: Literally, "properly"; so in this case, "when they don't fit in; when they don't do what's appropriate."

[26] Carnival is a period of balls and other merry-making that takes place before Lent.

[27] Jackson Haines (1840–1879) was a ballet master who moved to Vienna in 1863; in 1864, he "moved ballet to the ice and thus invented figure skating. He established schools in many countries, and his pupils took the idea all over the world." (Ralph Hickok, *Who Was Who in American Sports* [New York: Hawthorn Books, 1971], 124.)

[28] Elizabeth of Thuringia (1207–1231) was the daughter of the King of Hungary and was married at fourteen to the Landgrave of Thuringia. Very devout, she undertook acts of charity for the people of the land, both before and after her husband's death in 1227. She was canonized a few years after her death at twenty-four.

[29] Dutch: "Young lady; miss."

[30] August 15; a feast day that is observed in commemoration of the Assumption of the Virgin Mary.

[31] A fowling floor is a contraption that uses leafy branches, nets, and decoy-birds to trap wild fowl.

[32] These are characters in medieval German sagas. Siegfried and Kriemhild, husband and wife, are the male and female protagonists of the *Nibelungenlied*. The strong and heroic Siegfried is betrayed and murdered by his wife's family and their advisor; Kriemhild seeks revenge against them but is herself killed in the process. Isolde is the female protagonist of *Tristan*. She is married to Mark, although, thanks to a love potion, she is in love with Mark's friend and relative Tristan. Adultery follows.

[33] A style popular in early nineteenth-century France.

[34] Julius Benczur (1844–1920) was a Hungarian painter who did historical and genre paintings. He was also the portrait painter of the Hungarian aristocracy.

[35] The German is *Kappzaum*, which is a "lunging cavesson." A cavesson is a specialized type of bitless bridle. This particular cavesson is used for lunging, an activity in which the horse is driven around in a circle on a long line. The lunging cavesson is made more severe than an ordinary cavesson by the addition of a heavy jointed metal piece over the nose. Because it is heavy, it also tends to keep the horse's head down.